MW01295031

The Stick Horse Baby Cowboy

Cellulose John Wayne Jay

Peace. Love. Aloha.

Copyright © 2017 Cellulose John Wayne Jay
All rights reserved. No portion of this book my be reproduced or
transmitted in any form or by means without the prior written permission
of the author. ISBN:-10: 1979226342 ISBN-13: 978-1979226349

CHAPTER ONE

I, Cellulose John Wayne Jay, was born in the west in 1953, smack dab in the middle of the golden coast of California. My sister and I were very happy babies. My mother, Cleopatra, and my father, Abner Wingate Jay, moved our family to my maternal grandmother's house in Ohio when I was a very young boy. Ohio is where my baby sister, Francine, was born. What a beautiful baby she was. She was very loud and full of life. I was so excited as she was the first baby I had ever touched. I was going to get the chance to feed her, babysit her, hold her, and be her big brother. My older sister, Ann, and I watched as my mother prepared warm water for the baby's bath. "Pay attention," she said. "You and your big sister will have this job very soon."

That same day, my father said that when he returned from work, we would go to the park and play. In the meantime, I had work to do. We lived on the second-floor, and my grandmother lived on the first-floor. Mother sent me downstairs to help clean, and told me to stay out of trouble. I wanted to go out and play, but no one had the time. Grandmother said that maybe later we could play, and then she went upstairs to see the girls. I was left alone downstairs. What a big house it was! I went to the windows, but could not see outside. I went to the doors, but couldn't reach the door knobs. I went to the back of the house and removed a chair from the table. Now I could reach the knob. I twisted it open. Pure excitement ran through my body as I was outside in my grandmother's backyard. I looked around. I heard something. I wasn't sure of what I heard. I walked toward the sound. Freshly washed sheets were hanging on the clothesline. Careful not to touch the wash, I went between the sheets, then bent down low and crawled on my belly. I looked up and saw a big black dog and a little black and white dog. This was my first interaction with an animal. "John Wayne!" I heard my grandmother call out. She was not too happy to find me outside. She had forgotten to lock the back door after hanging out her morning wash. Had the door been dead-bolted, I would not have been able to get out. My hands were too small. "The big black dog will bite!" she yelled. It was too late. My

1

hand was already inside the fence. The dogs licked and slobbered all over my hands. I thought it was fun! Grandmother, my sister and Cleopatra stood behind me in total shock. Mother thought that for sure I would be torn apart. They were very bad dogs. Just a few days before, I had heard my grandfather, John Jay, say to his wife, "Thank God that the kid is not harmed!" Abner yelled out as he entered the backyard, "Let's all go inside! How did the boy get out near the dogs?" His mother took the blame right away, saying that she had forgotten to lock the door. As she prepared lunch, they all took turns speaking to me about the dangers of going outside without permission. "Please leave the dogs alone, Cellulose John Wayne Jay!" "Yes, grandfather. Yes, grandmother." I made it known to everyone that I would stay away from the killer dogs next door. As I started to eat, I thought to myself that surely, they must have been joking. I was just a kid, but I didn't think the dogs were that bad, and I knew for certain that I would touch them again.

After lunch, Abner took all of us kids to the park. What a fun day we had. I saw many kids and dogs. After a short time, it started to rain. Our play time was cut short, so we went home. My mother was taking a much needed time-out; she was sleeping. My father put Francine in the bed with our mother. Abner grabbed Ann and me by the hands and led us downstairs. He took us on a tour of the house which had many rooms. The last room we entered was the music room. It had lots and lots of instruments. My father was Abner Wingate Jay, known as the "Guitar Man." I had heard music before, but didn't understand where the sounds came from. Abner started to play a song. My sister and I fell asleep to beautiful music.

The next few days I stayed inside. No one had time to play. From the second-floor, I could see the dogs next door, and lots of kids all around. Suddenly, my mother called for me to help with the baby. It was time for me to hold little Francine. Everything was fine until she started to cry. My sister, Ann, took over. I asked my mother if I could sit in the window sill so that I could have a better view. She picked me up and sat me inside. What a view!

As the weeks and months passed, I was growing fast. I could reach all the door knobs. I thought about getting out. I wanted to touch the dogs next door again, but I knew my parents had said to stay away from them. A few nights after meeting the dogs, I couldn't sleep. All I could do was think about those dogs. Everyone in the house was asleep. I went downstairs and unlocked the door. I was very excited, and it was very dark. I tripped on the last step and fell in the mud. The dogs started to bark. I followed the sound. Then, I touched the fence. At that moment, I could see that the big black dog was on a chain. The little black and white dog was free. He ran to the fence and we touched. *How wonderful*, I thought, *that in just a few short months I had the pleasure of touching a newborn- Francine, my beautiful black baby sister, and two more of God's fabulous creatures- the dogs.* At that very moment, lights shined from next door and from my house. It was Abner, and I was busted! My daddy reached for my hand and picked me up. We walked over and talked to the man next door. Abner was very apologetic, and the dogs' owner said he didn't mind my interaction with his pets. He said that the dogs were new, and he was not sure if they would bite. With adventure in my face and in my voice, I said that the dogs sure had big teeth and eyes, but I didn't think they would bite me. I knew that teeth that size could tear me apart, but I thought the dogs just wanted to lick my hands. We said goodnight to the man with the dogs. My daddy was not too happy that I had gone outside at night, to see the dogs without permission. And he sure wasn't happy that I was a muddy mess. I undressed at the back door, so as not to track mud all over my granny's house. Abner gave me a bath and tucked me in. I dreamed of dogs that night.

The next day, I was sitting in the window sill, on the second-floor. I heard music. It wasn't my daddy. The sounds were getting closer. An unfamiliar creature with big black and white spots, was walking down the street, with a kid like me on its back. A man was leading it down the street. I gasped with excitement. Cleopatra ran to see what had caught my eyes. "It's a pony!" she said. I watched in amazement. The sound of hooves meeting pavement was sweet music to my ears. I asked my mother if I could go down to the street. "Not today," she said.

A few days later, I was in the window sill again. I saw the pony coming back down the street, but this time there was no kid on its back-just the man leading the pony. I waved my arms, wishing I could get his attention, but he didn't see me. My mother was in the bedroom with the girls. Grandmother was downstairs in her room. Grandfather was away, and Abner was working. The window was raised, and the only thing stopping me from climbing out, was the screen. I pushed, kicked, and then jumped out of the window from the second-floor. I fell into the hedge bush below the window. I was knocked out for a few seconds, then awakened by the licks and kisses from a big, red, sloppy tongue. It was the little black and white dog from next door. I could clearly see the black and white spotted pony disappearing around the corner. Darn it! I had missed that pony again! My parents were not happy. Once they realized I wasn't dead from the fall, I wasn't allowed near a door or window for awhile. They took my sisters and me to the doctor. The doctor told them that had it not been for the bush underneath the window, I may have broken my little cowboy neck. My mom started crying and screaming. I guess it just donned on her what had happened. "My kid just jumped out of a two-story window! Dr., is my boy crazy?" "Only horse-crazy, lady. Watch him closely. He may have a concussion. Bring him back to see me next week."

3

I got a good talking-to from my grandparents. They explained to me the dangers of being a hard-headed kid. "You could die long before your time. We love you, Cellulose John Wayne Jay. Now go to bed." The next day I felt fine. I could hear the dogs next door, but I did not get near a door or window. When Abner came home, we went to the music room for my first lesson. We had such a fun time. I just couldn't stop thinking about that pony.

CHAPTER TWO

Before I knew it, we were packing and leaving my grandmother's house. We drove from Ohio to Texas to meet my mama's folks. My two big aunties were there. It was love at first sight! Those gorgeous ladies were so much fun! I would love them all my life. One lived in Texas and the other lived in Arkansas. They raised my mother after her mom died and her father went to jail.

As we were driving, I saw lots of wonderful horses of all colors and sizes. Abner dropped us off in Texas. A few days later, my daddy went to Georgia- back to where he was born. My sisters and I didn't know about grown-up stuff. Abner and Cleopatra were going through a separation. There would be some sad times ahead.

I missed my daddy. My mother, two sisters and I lived in Texas for a few months. Then, we moved down south to where our aunt lived. We rode the train from Texas to Arkansas. That was my first train ride, and it was lots of fun. I was in horse heaven; on both sides of the tracks there were horses, dogs and cows. This was the first time I had laid eyes on a cow. "That's where milk comes from," my mom said. Once we arrived, my aunt took us around the circle to meet people. A dozen wonderful little old black ladies lived in the circle around my aunt's house We lived in a mixed community. Blacks and Whites got along fairly well. This was a very bad time in Arkansas, as far as race relations went. My sisters and I were thinking about school, but we knew about what had happened in Little Rock. Segregation was still around. My aunt was a former teacher, so we learned to read and write at a young age. My mother got a job. My aunt and all the little old ladies were our babysitters. What a fine time it was.

Across the street from our house there stood a big, three-story boarding house for Whites only. In front of the house was a fruit stand that took up the entire sidewalk, so there was always lots of action on the street. We lived with my aunt, and next door she had two boarding houses for Blacks only. Down the road and across the street, there was a fenced in lot with very, very tall trees and bushes. I heard sweet music again. It was the sound of hooves pounding. I said nothing. No one said anything to me about the ponies or horses across the street. I, being an investigator, had to check it out. Sure enough, there were horses inside that fenced lot. What a happy feeling I had.

All the sweet little old ladies in the circle had heard about my jumping out of the second-story window, in an attempt to catch a pony that I never did catch. I sat out front hoping to see someone checking on the horses. For weeks, no one came by. I looked inside the fence, and there was only dirt and weeds. This made me sad. One afternoon, I asked my mother in a round about way what horses eat. She told me they eat hay, grain, apples, carrots, and grass.

The following day I met the kid next door, who was much bigger than I, and already in school. He had also heard about my window incident in Ohio. The kid was impressed. He knew that I was either very courageous, very stupid, or just in love with a pony. He said, "I'm going to make it easy for you, Cellulose John Wayne Jay. You don't have to jump from a window. No one must know that you and I are going to climb one of the trees in the back. No one can see us. We'll walk until we find the right tree; one with branches that will help us to lower ourselves down into the horse pen. That's much better than jumping from the second-floor." *This time, I'm really going to catch a pony*! There are two horses inside. One is big and black, and the other is big and white. The kid tells me that they are plow horses, and I'm amazed at their size. The kid and I walked closer to the horses. They just stood still and let us touch them. I felt the same excitement as I did when I first touched baby Francine, and when the dogs licked my hand through the fence in Ohio. I was thrilled! It started to rain, so we cut our visit short. This was such a happy day. The kid said that he knew the owners of the horses, and that they would not be happy to find us inside the pen. He advised me not to go inside without him, because I was not a big boy yet, and I could get hurt. I said, "Sure, okay," but I didn't mean it. The kid next door liked horses, but he liked girls better.

The next day, my mother made me a stick horse from her old mop. I straddled the long handle, and held on to the head of the mop while walking and running. She picked up two beer cans and told me to step my feet into the middle of them and press down, until the ends of the cans fit tightly around the back of my feet. "Now you have shoes on your horse," she said. Off I rode, "click clack, click clack," down the sidewalk. It was not the sweet sound of hooves that I remembered on that Ohio street, but it was close enough.

I was riding my stick pony down the sidewalk when three of the little old ladies were out in their yards. "Nice pony, cowboy!" "Thanks, ladies!" "John Wayne, we're going to get right to the point. Kids before you have gotten hurt real bad, and gotten into lots of trouble for hanging around those horses- for trespassing. We know the owner, and he's not real nice. Be careful. We ladies have a job for you. We have already talked it over with your mother. Here's a list. Go across the main road to the store. Watch for cars. Take this five dollars, and you can keep the change." Now that's how I met the little old ladies. They were impressed that I could read, write, and count at the age of four. After shopping, I had one dollar left. I went across to the White boarding house where the fruit stand was located, and purchased apples and carrots for the big horses across the road. Sure, I had been warned to stay away, but for some reason, I didn't hear so well. I was sitting on my bed, with a bag of apples and carrots. I was thinking that my big sister was asleep, but she wasn't. She wanted an update on my activities. She was happy that I was now working for the sweet little old ladies. My mother, baby sister, and aunt were all asleep. Ann said to me, "I know what you're going to do." I gave her two apples, and she fell asleep. I was going to wait until morning to feed the horses, but I just couldn't wait that long. The moon was out and I could see very well. I didn't want to climb the tree or the fence to enter the pen. I was in the back of the pen, and the dirt around the fence bottom was very soft. I started digging with my hands, a rock, and some sticks. I went under the fence. I was inside! I had never fed a pony before, so I started to eat. I took a big bite from one of the apples. The horses walked slowly to my outreached hand. There was contact. The apple disappeared. The horse wanted another. The white pony just stood there. I tried to give him an apple, but he dropped it. So, I gave him a carrot, which he seemed to like better. Clouds were about to block the moon. It was getting dark fast. I couldn't find my way out, so I followed the fence bottom until I found the trench that led me out. That was my first time trespassing all by myself. It was thrilling! I ran home and everyone was still sleeping.

The next day was my mother's day off, and she took us kids shopping. It was my first trip downtown, and it was a happy day. *Thank you, Lord.* My mother treated us to ice cream cones. When we arrived back home, there was a man in the yard talking with my aunt. What really caught my eye was the biggest dog I had ever seen. "I'm Reverend Jones," the man said, "and this is one of my pets. His name is Samson." Once again, I am witnessing another one of God's magnificent creatures! "He's a Great Dane. Would you like to take a ride, Cellulose John Wayne Jay?" "Yes, sir, I would!" Most Sunday afternoons he would let the kids ride Samson. What excitement! I looked over to my left at my stick pony standing against the house. "Hope you don't mind," I said to my stick pony, "but this is as close as I've ever come to riding a real pony!" Those horses across the street were so big compared to this Great Dane, and I wondered how I would get onto their backs. Oh well, first things first. I mounted Samson with the help of Reverend Jones. To this day, I can still feel the excitement that I felt when the Great Dane took his first steps with me aboard. I was thrilled! Words really can't express how I felt in that moment. You'll just have to take my word for it. Samson, the Reverend Jones and I rode down the sidewalk to the little sweet old ladies' house. "Howdy, John Wayne! Looks like fun!" the ladies yelled. "I wish we could ride!" one of the ladies added, with a big smile on her face.

I was up early the next morning, and to my surprise, a big truck was going inside the gate across the street where the big horses lived. Once the gates were closed, I could not see inside. So, I went behind the house, to where men had been working on my aunt's roof the day before. They had left the ladder leaning against the house. I climbed on top to get a better look. I could see them taking the big black horse, and leaving the big white one in the pen. This was the first human movement I had seen in the horse pen. *The big White cowboy must be the owner*, I thought. The horses walked right up to him, and he didn't have an apple or carrots, nor did he have any hay. The man loaded the horse into the truck and drove away. I wondered if I would ever see that pony again. Water was now all that Big White had in the pen. I was sad. I went to Cleopatra and said, "Mother, I confess, I went over to visit the horses when you said not to." "Yes, cowboy, I know." I had been warned many times to stay away, but like they say, those warnings "went in one ear and out the other." My mother didn't spank me. She just said, "Be as careful as you can, son."

The sweet old ladies called for me the next day. Nine of the dozen little old ladies needed items from the store. I helped them for most of the day. I made about four trips across the main road. They made lunch and we sat and talked. That's when they told me that five of them were ex-cowgirls. Now most of these girls were well into their eighties, but their minds were still very sharp, and they still had many fond memories of cowgirl days. Those days were gone forever in a physical sense, but in their minds, they knew that, through me, they could all ride again. When my aunt told them about my jumping out of the window trying to catch a pony, and then they saw me riding atop the Great Dane- they knew I was their cowboy. The ladies were well aware of my trespassing in the horse pen. I'm thinking that my mother told them. One of the little old sweet ladies said to me, "John Wayne, we can tell you anything you want to know about ponies, horses, donkeys, burros or a jack ass. Now kid, tell us, some of us are missing mops and brooms. Would you, baby cowboy, know anything about that?" "Yes, ma'am, I would. The mops and brooms looked old and worn out, so I made a few stick horses, and one stick horse is for a new pal of mine.

CHAPTER THREE

I met a kid on the way to the store the other day. His name is Rex. He lives behind the store, across the main road from my house. Sometimes, when I have small items to buy, I ride my stick pony with beer cans on my feet, "click clack, click clack," up and down the road- sweet music to my ears- almost like real horse hooves, with real horse shoes. Rex saw me. As we got close, our eyes met. He was the first white boy I had ever seen. We talked. He loved my pony. I asked him if he would like to ride. I walked, and he rode my stick pony for about a block, until we got to the store. I went inside to shop for two of the ladies while Rex waited outside with the pony. "No horses inside!" the store owner yelled. I purchased five penny cookies. Rex and I sat on the side of the store to eat our cookies. Rex told me that he had never met a black boy before. I was the first. I told him that he was the first white kid I had met. He said he thought his father hated black people. I asked him why.

The little old ladies didn't care that I had made stick horses out of their mops. In fact, they loved it. I told them I had a new pal, and that he was a white boy. They were thrilled for us, but were also a little concerned for our safety. There was a great amount of tension in the air during this time- racial tension, which is the worst kind. Many white people didn't want the black kids to swim at the White pool. Most kids just want to have fun and swim in a big pool. I'm four-years-old, and Rex is five-and-a-half. He's a bigger boy, and is already in school- preschool he told me. And he would like to have some black classmates.

CHAPTER FOUR

"Cellulose John Wayne Jay, we know that one horse is left in the pen," the sweet little old lady cowgirls said to me. "We also know that nothing is going to stop you from riding that horse. We can help you stay safe. How do you plan on getting atop such a tall horse?" "I'm not sure," I answered. They wanted to know how I enter the pen. "I enter either over the fence, or under the fence." "Tie the pony to the tree. We've got a rope." I said "Sure," but that I wasn't sure how to catch him. "With a carrot in hand, he should walk right up to you. Put the rope around his neck. It will be easy. Just do it, cowboy." "Yes, ladies," I answered. I am wondering why there is no food for the pony. I asked the ladies and they all looked puzzled. "Look Cellulose John Wayne Jay, we are going to send you on a little mission. You know the Hobo Trail out behind the horse pen- we want you to go and cross the bridge, turn left down the railroad tracks, walk two blocks, and turn right. There are four big warehouses full of hay. When the men unload the trucks, they always drop lots of hay on the ground. We have a bag for you."

The next day I got the hay. Oh what a happy day! *Thank you, Lord. God doesn't make mistakes.* I was so excited as I was running down the railroad tracks with the bag filled to the top with hay. All the while I was thinking how happy the pony is going to be at dinner time. I'm crossing the bridge, running down the Hobo Trail, when two old white hobos stopped me. "We've been watching you for some time now, and we're going to help you." They took the bag and the rope, then one of the hobos lifted me onto his shoulders, and dropped me over the fence, into the pen. Only one of the hobos climbed inside the pen with me. The other man was too drunk, so he was the look-out man. We did not want to get into trouble for trespassing. The very nice hobo walked right up to the pony and put the rope around his neck. We let Big White eat his newfound dinner. He was happy and so was I. God must have been happy, as well. I never knew the names of the hobos, but I thanked them. "Anytime, kid," they said. After dinner, the man put me aboard the horse and led me around, just like

Reverend Jones did when I rode Samson, the Great Dane. "Kid, the best way for you to ride this big, tall white horse is to tie him to this tree and gently slide out of the tree, onto his back." He showed me how to make a rope halter and reins. He rode the horse around for awhile. Then, it was my turn. My first horseback ride- excitement filled my whole body. What a legendary moment in the life of a baby cowboy! The next day the ladies called for me. They wanted a cowboy update. "Did you get the hay? Did you catch the pony? Did you tie him to the tree and drop down from the tree branch onto his back?" They were more excited than I, it seemed. The little sweet old lady cowgirls were living out their last days through me, and they were so very happy. As time passed, I found out that the owner of the horses across the street had passed away, and the horses and the land had been sold. I thought I would never see Big White and Big Black again.

CHAPTER FIVE

My big sister loves school. She's telling me about things she's learning and the new kids she is meeting. I wish I could go to school, but I have to wait one more year. Right now I have to spend more time with my baby sister. My mother said that today we are going to move into a bigger house around the corner. "Start packing," she said. Two of the sweet little old lady cowgirls' kids were coming to take them away, up north somewhere, and two of the ladies had passed away to Cowgirl Heaven. We were all sad. Eight ladies were left. They called me over, and told me that the thoroughbreds were coming to town. "What's that?" I asked. "Wonderful race horses," they said to me, "and it's going to take time to explain all of this. First of all, there is a racetrack five miles down the road. Cleopatra will take you someday."

I went home to talk to my mom. She sent me around the corner to talk to my aunt. My aunt then took me next door to her rooming house. She checked all the rooms to make sure that they were clean. "Cellulose John Wayne Jay, I am going to have lots of race trackers here next week. They take care of the race horses, and I'm going to send you to work with these old Black cowboys some mornings. How would you like that, kid?" "I would love it. Thank you, ma'am." "Okay kid, you can get on your stick pony now. I need you to shop for me." I wanted to ride past my new pal Rex's house, which is behind the store. He's still the only white kid I know, and I haven't seen him in a long time. I finish shopping and get back to my aunt's house. She is very happy. She's talking to my daddy, Abner Wingate Jay, over the phone. She hands me the phone. He says it's over with Cleopatra. He now has a new wife and a new life, but wants me to be on the look out, because he is going to come and get us kids, and drive us to Georgia for the summer. "Yes, sir," I said. I gave the phone back to my aunt. I went home and told my mother and sisters about the phone call. Everyone was happy.

It's almost Christmas and it's getting cold outside. I look down the road, and here comes Reverend Jones with one of his pets. I wanted to ride, but I had to help mother work around the house. Lots of new kids are coming around to ride the Great Danes. I go to my aunt's house the next morning. There are lots of men and trucks across the street in the horse pen. My pal, Rex, is walking down the sidewalk. He's never crossed the main road before. He has great news. His father left home and he has a new father who loves all people, and has a pony that Rex and I can ride. Pure excitement runs through my body. My pal's new father will also be working in the horse pen that was sold. It will become a new shopping center.

The sweet little old ladies call for me the next day. I make three trips across the main road to shop. There is lots of action all around. The race trackers are in town. I'm standing on the corner and many horse vans pass by, with the horses' heads in the windows, as if to say, "Hello!" I rush back from the store. The ladies and I have lunch. They want a cowboy update. A total of four cowgirls have passed away, and the remaining ladies just want to talk. All the other kids are in school. My baby sister and I are the only kids the little ladies spend time with. They really love us. We love them, too. They know that I will soon be getting a chance to be on the racetrack. "Stay alert and pay attention. Lots of action is on the track, kid. Stay safe!" Three days later, I met the race trackers. I said, "Wranglers, I'm going with you cowboys in the morning." The men looked at me with happy eyes and said, "Your aunt informed us two weeks ago, John Wayne. Get some sleep, kid. We are up at three in the morning."

I tossed and turned. I couldn't sleep. I thought about the pony that got away in Ohio, the stick horses, the Great Dane rides, and the big white horse across the street. *Thank you, Lord.* The next morning came fast. When we got close to the track, I laid down on the floor in the back of the truck, so as not to be seen by the guard at the front gate. Kids were not allowed in the barns, or anywhere on the backside. But I was with some old Black legendary cowboys, wild horse wranglers extraordinaire, pony boys, out riders, grooms and two Black jockeys. I thought it was interesting that everybody on the backside of the track was black. The only white people I saw were the owners and trainers. We went to each stall. "Clean all water buckets and put in fresh water," the cowboys told me. The men rolled the feed cart down the middle of the barn and we started feeding horses. They were magnificent thoroughbreds. The horses eat and drink while men clean their stalls. After the stalls are cleaned, the hot walkers go to work walking horses around the barn. Now we're waiting to find out how many horses are going to the track for training work outs. "Let's get them ready!" the boss yells. I looked down the barn, and saw the jockeys coming toward me. They said good morning to me and wanted to know if I was a jockey in training. I said, "No, sir, I'm just looking to learn." "Stick around, kid, you'll learn plenty." All the grooms had about one hundred safety pins stuck to their pants for wrapping legs with cotton rags. We were all done by ten o'clock. The cowboys return at three o'clock to feed dinner. Three days a week I was on the racetrack. What a life! *Thank you, Lord, and please bless all of my newfound pals- the race horses!* Later that night, I had dinner with the cowboys and they were thrilled with my work. "Goodnight, cowboys. See you day after tomorrow."

The next day is my mother's day off from work. She is washing and brushing my sisters' hair. She says my hair is next, and that she is going to cut it off. After three hours of grooming, Cleopatra took a power nap. She was worn out from a six-day work week. My big sister was doing her school work. She's so smart and beautiful. My baby sister's hair is long, black and shiny, and in two pony tails down to her waist. Her little face is black and beautiful. I love my sisters. For some reason, just out of the blue, I picked up the cutters and cut one of my sister's pony tails off, almost up to her neck. I picked it up off the floor. She saw what I had done and started to cry, then scream and yell. My mother heard the screams and came into the room. Francine is standing in the middle of the room, crying and holding a two-foot-long pony tail. My mother went crazy! "Cellulose John Wayne Jay, what have you done, boy? She ran toward me and I ran for the front door. I ran fast like a race horse! Cleopatra was running, trying to catch me, but there was no way that she could. I ran down to my aunt's house and told her what happened. "Cleo is going to kill me!" I said. "No, she's not," she answered. My aunt went outside to talk to my mama, but Cleo was not in the talking mood. She yelled out to me, "John Wayne, you might belong to God, but your ass belongs to me!" "Cleo, go home," my aunt said, "because in your state of mind you could hurt this boy. He didn't mean to do it." "I want him out of my house!" Cleo yelled. "John Wayne is my boy right now. He stays with me," my aunt said. "The baby's hair will grow back fast." Cleo didn't have any clear understanding about what I had just done. My mother was very mad and didn't want to see me. I had to stay at my aunt's house for one year. The legendary baby cowboy got kicked out of the house at the age of five. The next day, everybody heard what had happened. No one was mad, except Cleopatra. My mother dropped Francine off with the little old ladies and went to work. She passed by my aunt's house, but didn't stop to say hello. My big sister stopped on her way to school, and said that she and Francine were not mad at me. "We love you, John Wayne," she said. "Peace."

The construction has started across the street and there is lots of action. I sit in front of the house most of the day watching the big dump trucks and heavy equipment. My aunt is taking me to Bible study later today with Reverend Jones. Maybe I'll see the Great Danes. My new pal, Rex, is walking down the sidewalk. He's with another white kid. His name is Billy Bob, and he's another kid with some horses. They want to know if I can come along and ride. My aunt went outside to talk to the boys. When they saw her, they thought she was a white lady. She is very light skinned, and all the white people thought she was a white lady with black friends. There was lots and lots of racial tension at this time, during the 1950's. My pals Rex and Billy Bob were very brave boys. My aunt said to the boys, "I'll need to talk with your parents." Rex told my aunt that his father worked across the street and could come talk to her at noon. What a happy day. Thank you, Lord. Everything went well. My aunt said I could go with the boys to ride that following week.

After Bible study with Reverend Jones, we went three blocks over to my aunt's church. She is the only Black person who is a member of an all-White congregation. When we walked in, the people were in a state of shock. The pastor informed us that no Blacks were allowed. My aunt said to the pastor, "I have been a member here for ten years." The pastor said, "Lady, I didn't know that you were Black. The congregation is not going to be happy." My aunt had tears in her eyes. She said, "I thought that we were all God's children." We left for home and she cried most of the way. I had never seen my aunt cry before. It was a very sad day.

CHAPTER SIX

"John Wayne, I'm going to take you to town with me in the morning and show you how to pay my bills. You can pay the light, gas and water bills for me and then we can get some ice cream. I know you need to go with the cowboys in the morning- but I need you.

Most of my little old lady cowgirls are dead now. Only six ladies are left in the circle. I miss the ones that are gone. I miss the six girls who are still here, because I don't see them as much these days. They are slowing down and don't need as much, but once a week they get a cowboy update, we still have lunch, and we're still in love.

Last night I dreamed about Cleopatra. Early in the morning my aunt and I head downtown. My aunt said to all the shop owners, "This is Cellulose John Wayne Jay. He is my brother's grandson. He lives in my house with me, and he will be paying my bills if I can't make it down here." The people were in a state of shock. All of these years they thought my aunt was a white lady. This was my first time deep in the city. It was a very hot day and there was lots of excitement. It was the 1950's in the deep south of Arkansas, and some stores didn't allow black kids to enter without a parent. It appears as though I am walking down the street holding a white lady's hand. We got lots of bad looks, but we also get lots of smiles. I look across the street. I see my mother. She sees us and comes over. She gives me a hug and a kiss and tells me she loves me. She says she isn't mad anymore and that she's on her lunch break. She is shopping for my sisters and wants to buy Francine a new doll. She thought I should pick out the doll so I could give it to my sister and tell her I was sorry for the hair cut. All of the dolls are white. They all look alike, until I walked down a few more steps. I ask mother, "What about this one? Who is she?" "She's a China doll. A doll from China," Cleo answered. "Where is this place?" I asked. "Far, far away." "Where are the black dolls?" "There are no black dolls here." Cleo answered. So my sisters and I were meeting China for the first time. Francine was so happy to meet her new doll. She kissed me, and said that she was never mad at me and that she loved me.

16

I'm going to see thoroughbreds in the morning, and sweet little ladies in the afternoon. The cowboys are up next door. I hear them talking. They will be calling me soon. My aunt is up early. I wonder why. She's never up this early. She wants to let me know that my mother and sisters are moving about ten blocks away, across from the school, but she needs me to help her around the house. She has three houses. There's always something to do around the place. I'm still too young for school. Next year is my year.

The cowboys and I get to the racetrack, and as we get out of the car, people start yelling, "Loose horse! Loose horse!" It' dark and hard to see, but I hear hooves, "click clack, click clack." "Watch out, kid, he's coming your way!" I step into the road and the horse stops right at my feet. I reach up and catch the rope. Men come running from all directions. They are amazed to see a kid hold on to all that power. They thanked me and walked off in the dark to the other side of the track. I start cleaning and filling the water tubs with fresh water. One of the pony boys said that he would let me ride his horse anytime I could. The other great news is that I am going to be helping the grooms wrap legs this morning. The cart is coming with the feed. The horses are very excited. Everyone is going to the track this morning. The jockeys are in the barn and there is lots of action every day. The mornings go by very fast. There's a lot to do, and lots of teamwork.

I rush home after working on the track. The church calls my aunt to say that, "Blacks can come and pray, and we hope you want to stay." The next Sunday my aunt took her friend to church and all was well. *God doesn't make mistakes, but people do.* The ladies need me today. I'm always happy to see and help them. They want to know about Rex and Billy Bob, as well as my great day on the track. After shopping, we talked and had lunch. I'm going over to my mother's new house today. I hope to see my big sister playing outside in the school yard when I pass by. The new house is across the street from the school. There are lots of kids in this part of town. I don't know many kids my age, but I will next year, when I start school.

My father is back to take my sisters and me to his hometown in Georgia. We will be away for six months. What a happy day! I run next door to say thank you to the cowboys for taking me on the racetrack and teaching me about horses. They said, "Glad to help, kid. See you next year." Then I ran down the street to the little old ladies' house. They are very sad to see me go, but happy because I have my daddy back with me. I missed him very much. Cleopatra is happy, also. My aunt and mother are leaving for Texas to see my aunt's sister, who is not feeling so well. Maybe one day I will get a chance to go back to Texas and ride some wild horses. I went across the street to see if I could find Rex's daddy. I see his truck, but he's not around. I want to let him know that I still want to ride when I come back to town in six months.

The next day we hit the road for a long drive. I saw lots of horses and cows on both sides of the road. This is only my second time taking a long car trip. It's like driving from my grandmother's Ohio home to Texas, then to Arkansas. I love to go places. There's always lots to see. My baby sister is starting to cry. She wants her mother. We want to know from Abner all about his wife- our new step-mother. "What's her name?" "Doll Baby, and you're going to love her. She's very nice." Abner said we can all go to school. Francine and I have never been to school, but we sure would like to. We fall asleep. When we wake up, we see our new mother for the first time, and we know we are going to love her. She seems so nice. We go inside the very big house. Doll Baby makes lunch for us. She tells us all about the school. We went shopping later that day, and looked around the town. My daddy and his new wife are happy. The next week we went to school to look around. Oh, what a happy day! Everyone has the same light blue and dark blue uniforms. That sweet Doll Baby made our uniforms. We are so happy and we thank her every day. Abner took us to meet some of our kin folks across town. There were lots of horses everywhere, on both sides of the roads. I saw a little black boy on his pony; something I'd never seen in my hometown. I asked Abner if he knew any black horse owners in town. "Lots." he said. "I'll take you one day to ride some horses."

Time moved along very fast. Before we knew it, we were in school. What a thrill! The Guitar Man- my daddy, Abner Wingate Jay, kept his promise to us kids. He said he would come back to get us, and he did just that. *Thank you, Lord.* We're having a great time in school, meeting lots of new kids, and learning lots of new things. My father and new mother are music people- song writers with keyboards and vocals. My mother and Abner played about ten instruments. Some of the instruments were from the mother country of Africa. I started to play with the guitars. They were all over the house. Doll Baby taught us how to sing and pay attention. She was a great story teller. She loved us as if we were her own kids. We learned a lot of songs in a short amount of time. Before we knew it, we were performing in church. My sisters and I loved to sing and we were good at it. My daddy was born and raised in Georgia, and was a Guitar Man all his life. We met many of my father's musical pals. Some would make it very big in the music world- from Georgia all the way to the top of the charts. *Thank you, Lord, for the great time we're having in Georgia.*

Cleopatra called today to tell us that she loved us and to be good kids, and to hurry back home. We miss our mother and aunt. I think of my little old sweet lady cowgirls- the ones now in heaven and the ones left in the circle back in my hometown. I pray for them every night. I remember the things they told me. My aunt also said that my white boy pals have been coming around looking for me. They miss me and can't hardly wait for my return. "We've got horses to ride, country to see, and new people to meet," they said to my aunt. She gave the boys apple pie and thanked them for stopping over. The boys are working across the street with their fathers on the new shopping center- the ex-horse pen, the place where I rode my first pony. My aunt also said that the race trackers missed me and wished me well.

Time moved fast for us. Before we knew it, we were back home in Arkansas. My sisters cried with joy. They were so happy to see Cleopatra and our aunt. After being home a day or two, I went back across the main road to my aunt's house, about ten blocks away. She was so glad to see me, and told me that she loved me. The next day, I wanted to see if I could help the little old sweet ladies. They, too, were happy to see me. They sent me to the new shopping center across the street. What a large store it was! I walked around looking for items, thinking to myself how Big White and Big Black, the first ponies I ever rode, once lived here. They didn't live here anymore, but they would always live in my heart and in my mind. *Thank you, Lord.* I paid for my items and ran back across the street to the ladies. We talked and had lunch, with cowboy updates.

The weekend is here, and Rex and Billy Bob are outside with their fathers. We are going horseback riding and maybe for a swim. I don't know how to swim. When we got to the ranch, my eyes opened wide with excitement. The first two horses I saw were Big White and Big Black. I was so glad to see them again! I didn't know that Billy Bob's father owned the first pony I had ever ridden. I never got the chance to ride Big Black, so today, I wanted to ride him first. The fathers got three horses ready, and we rode in the big round pen for two hours. I was having so much fun and I didn't want to stop riding Big Black.

The boys' mothers came outside to meet me. *Very nice ladies*, I thought. They made lunch for us and we talked. They really made me feel welcomed. After lunch, we gave the horses a bath and some hay. *Next time I'll ride Big White.* The father took us down to the swimming hole behind the barn. Rex and Billy Bob are great swimmers. I've only been to the Black pool in town. It's very small, and there's always lots of kids, and not enough room to really learn how to swim. The boy's daddy picked me up and tossed me into about five feet of water. When I came up to the top, they said, "Kick your feet and pull the water back to your body in a round motion." I went under water a few times and drank a little water, but I was swimming. After going back to the ranch, the boys' parents said they loved having me over to play with the boys. I'm the first black kid that their kids ever met. I was welcome to come to the ranch anytime and ride. The ranch is about ten miles outside town. They said, "Cellulose John Wayne Jay, if no one is home, you go in the barn and get a pony and ride." I thanked them for their kindness. They drove me back home in the truck. "There's a bike in the truck bed. It's yours, kid." the father said. "Ride out and see us anytime." *What a blessed day. Thank you, Lord.* Before they drove off, I asked the fathers to let everyone know that a black boy will be coming around, and not to call the police. I won't be trespassing.

My aunt was glad that I had a great time with my new white pals. They know I'm black and they don't care- unlike my aunt's all-White church. We're eating when my aunt tells me that one of the little old ladies passed away today, while I was out with Rex and Billy Bob. I asked if I could go over to see Cleopatra and my sisters. She told me I could, and as I walked, I thought of the first time I met all the sweet old ladies and how now, there are only four left. Oh how I miss them- dead or alive. My mother and the kids are very glad to see me. I'm glad to see them as well. A cowboy update is what they need. My sisters don't like horses. They like dolls. Cleo tells me I'll be going across the street to school very soon. She wants me to stay home. She misses me and wants to take me to school in the morning. She wants to look around and size the place up. I'm almost six-years-old now. I'm thinking of all the new kids I'm going to meet. My mother is happy that I went for a pony ride and a swim. The next day my big sister went to class. Cleo, my baby sister and I looked around the school. There were lots of kids. I knew I would love this Goldstein School House.

The White boarding house, across the street from my aunt, has a fruit and vegetable stand in the front of the house. The owner has passed away and his wife would like the big kid who lives next door to my aunt, and me, to work for her, selling fruit and vegetables. The next week we went out on the road about ten miles outside of town. She helped us boys set up, and left us there for half a day. When she returned, everything was sold. I saw horses in the field behind the stand. I thought to myself, *The next time I'm here, I will go over for a better look.* She tells us she needs us to work three days a week, and we tell her it's a sure thing. We can do this. We drive home and she pays us five dollars.

After being home for an hour or so, I went around the corner to check on the little old ladies. There is only time to sit and talk. They wanted a cowboy update. They were excited that I would be going to Goldstein school. The next day, my pal Rex called to tell me that his family bought a new house outside of town. He was happy to tell me that a black kid lives next door, and that he went over to meet the boy and his parents. Rex is glad to know that he is going to go to school with black kids. They didn't want to be like Little Rock.

Time's moving fast and school is about to start. The big boy next door is not feeling well, so he can't go to work today. I told the boss lady to let me go and work alone. I could set up and run the fruit stand by myself. We loaded up the truck, and out to the country we drove. It's Sunday morning and not many cars are on the roads. We get to the stand, set up everything, and sit and talk. When she leaves, I decide to go see if I can find horses behind the stand. An hour had gone by, and no one had stopped to buy fruit, so I decided it was a good time to scout for ponies. I've been thinking about these ponies. I walk down the hill to the trees and see movement. I hear something. It's a cow. I've seen cows before, but not this near to me. I didn't know the sounds they made; it sounded like the cow was singing to me. I move along down into the trees and, lo and behold, the best thing I've seen all morning is looking me right in the face- six horses! One of them is hurt. He has a rope wrapped around his legs and is unable to move. I had to think and move fast. I ran from the trees and fast up the grass hill to the fruit stand. There was a box cutter I used to open the fruit crates. I grabbed it and started back down the hill when a car pulled up. It was a lady wanting to buy fruit. As soon as she left, I got back to the pony. I cut him free, and he ran off fast with his pals. They were very happy. I stayed and watched as they ran far over the grass hill, bucking and kicking and looking swell. When I got back to the fruit stand, someone had left twenty dollars, and a note listing the items they had removed from the stand. After church, lots of people came by, and before I knew it, the fruit was sold out. The boss lady would be happy.

All the big boys on my street are joining the boy scouts. I'm not old enough to join. We don't have cub scouts for black kids- only boy scouts. My mother's going to contact the scouts and find out if black kids are welcome to join the white cub scout troop. She says she doubts it, but it's worth a try.

It was around this time when I had my first trip to the dentist. Mother and I walked downtown. It was a very, very hot day. We stopped to get cold drinks about half way there. We sat in the park to drink them, and I asked Cleo why we were going to the dentist. She said I needed a check up. In the fifties, there was only one dentist that would treat Blacks in my town. We got to the office on the tenth-floor. It was a very long and hot walk up the stairs. Sometimes we could not ride the elevator. I sat in the chair and the dentist pulled out a long needle. When I saw this, I started to move, and the man slapped me in the face and told me to stay still. Cleopatra just lost it. She ran over to the chair and slapped the dentist about three times, grabbed my hand, and we ran ten-floors down the back stairs into the first-floor lobby. When we stepped out onto the street, the police were in front of the office. They talked to my mother and then put us in the back of the police car. It was very hot. I asked the police if he could roll down the window, but he said no. A lady walked by who knew Cleo, and told her she would call our aunt. The cops went inside to talk with the dentist. Just as they returned, my aunt jumped out of a taxi. She walks everywhere, but today she took a cab because she knew my mother had a bad temper, and could be in lots of trouble. When the police saw my aunt, they smiled and said hello. My aunt said, "Hello, officer, this lady works for me." They opened the door and let us out. The police knew my aunt from her boarding houses. She has called them many times over the years. They think my aunt is a white lady. That's why we went free. The next week my mother took me to the big city of Little Rock for a dentist appointment. I didn't get slapped, but I still had to face the long needle. It wasn't so bad.

Time's moving fast and I'm going to school next week. I'm very excited. I've met lots of new kids at mother's new house across from the school. I've also met some kids from Ann's class. She's in the second grade, and loves school. A few days before school begins, my aunt gets a call from her friend. Her friend is going fishing in the morning and she would like to come by and take us with her. While fishing the next day, I caught my first fish. What a thrill! This is something that I wish I could do every day, but we live a long way from the lake, and we don't drive.

Today was the last day to go swimming at the Black pool. Lots of the big boys went to the White pool to see if they could enter. They were told, "Not at this time." The boys left, and went back much later and jumped the fence to take a swim. As they were leaving, people yelled at them and called them names that I won't repeat. The boys were just trying to have a nice swim.

Cleopatra is taking us to the movies today to see Elvis for the first time. I'm very excited. We go downtown, and the movie house is showing something we don't want to see, instead of Elvis. They tell us Elvis is showing uptown, and that uptown does not cater to Black people at this time. As they smiled, we walked away disappointed. In my town, we had three movie houses and one drive-in movie. Blacks and Whites could go together at one house, but Blacks had to sit up top, and Whites sat downstairs. The rest of the movie houses were for Whites only.

The next day, the Guitar Man, Abner Wingate Jay- my daddy, sent three guitars from Georgia to my aunt's house. My sisters gave me all the guitars. They don't want to play. They like dolls. I stayed up half the night making lots of noise. The next morning I'm up early- I've got to walk to my mama's house. She's taking me to school this morning. I'm going to be in the first grade at Goldstein. We go inside the office and take a seat. There are lots of people, and time passes slowly. Finally, they call my name. Cleo and I go into the main office. They tell my mother that since my birthday is in November, I can't go to school until next year. Man, I am so sad. I sit on the front steps, and watch all my pals walk by on their way to school.

My mother comes outside to tell me that she's going to have a baby, and she wants me to know that I will not be cutting anymore hair.

I went home to my aunt's house. Shortly after I got there, Billy Bob's father called to tell us that he had bad news. His son fell in the mud through a wooden fence while riding his pony. The doctors said he is going to live, but he may not walk again. I want to go see my pal but his father said that next week would be better. I thought about the pony. "How is Big White?" I asked. "Big White's leg was broken and he had to be put down." The first horse I ever rode is dead, and one of my very first white baby cowboy pals is hurt badly. My other white pal, Rex, called me. We were both sad as we talked about Billy Bob. Rex and his father are going to pick me up in a few days and take me to their ranch to ride a pony, and maybe to visit our pal. We miss him and we pray for him. I find out later the kid's arm is broken, a rib is broken, a leg is broken and he is black and blue all over. I know Billy Bob's daddy said I could visit next week, but for some reason, I don't think so. I only hope so. The kid is in a lot of pain.

I tell Rex that I can't go to school until next year. He is sad for me. He tells me black kids are going to his new school, and he has already made friends with them all. He is excited, and has told them about how he and I met, and how I gave him my first stick pony.

The big kid next door is calling for me to come outside and play. His mother has told him that I won't be going to school this year. He is sad for me. We used to talk about how we would soon be walking to school together with the other kids. I'm the only kid that's not in school around the circle. My pal also wants to tell me of the new horses that are not far from our house. Maybe I can walk down the railroad tracks and take a look one day. I'm sure that I will, now that I know where they are located. He also tells me that our boss lady with the fruit stand has passed away. This is sad news. We loved that lady. She took a big chance on us kids by letting us run her fruit and vegetable stand out in the country after her husband passed away. My pal says that maybe I could help him at his new job at the shopping center across the street from our house where the horse pen once stood- the place where Big White and Big Black once lived. I inform him that Big White is dead, and that no one rides Big Black, and that the owner's kid is hurt. We reflect back to the day that we went around behind the pen to see the horses. My pal tells me he really loves school. His grades are great, he says. I wish I could go. His new job is helping the truck driver unload food and other items in the store at night. He tells me that our parents must not know. "Sure," I say.

The next day my aunt needs me to help her around the house. She is going to let a single mother and her two kids move into the rooming house. This has never been done before. Her house rules, *Men Only*, were no more. She said she had to help this lady and her kids. We must move a few things around and make sure the place is clean. My aunt made it clear that they could stay until the race trackers return in three to four months.

I make a call to Billy Bob's house, but no one picks up. My aunt says I can go out and play. I go behind the shopping center, down by the creek, through the Hobo Trail, and across the bridge to the train tracks. I walk about five miles. I have never walked this far in this direction before. I see horses up the hill to my right. I stop to drink from my canteen. I look across the tracks and there are more horses. My heart starts to beat faster. I am excited about what I see. It's a long walk, but well worth it. All together, I see about nine horses and five cows. I don't see any people, houses or trucks. *Go for it, baby cowboy*! I get near the fence and I go under. I have two carrots and a small, thin rope in my pocket. I catch one horse and move off into the bush. When the other horses joined us, the two carrots had already been eaten. I didn't have more carrots, and I did not want to get stepped on, so I left. I went across the tracks, to find the horses I saw behind the trees. I see them, but they are too far way. *Maybe next time, I have to be getting back home. It's a very long walk, and it might rain.* When I made it back home, my mother and sisters were all there.

I called Billy Bob's house again. This time someone picks up- it's his mother and she is glad that I called. She says her son is much better, and he wants to see me. "I'll come and get you, baby cowboy. I'll come Monday since you're not in school. Rex was here last night, and he told us of you not being able to go to school this year." She wanted to talk to my aunt. They spoke a little bit. After they said goodnight, my aunt tells my mother and me that Billy Bob's mother is selling all the horses.

After we eat, my mother and the girls go home. I fall asleep, and then the kid next door starts tapping on my window. I wake up, and jump out of the window- ground floor this time. We run across the street. The food truck is coming down the road. We help the driver for about an hour, one night a week. He pays us five dollars each. I run home and fall back to sleep. The next day, I meet the two kids and their mother. They are moving into my aunt's rooming house next door. They are of school age, and their mother tells me that the kids will be going to school next week. I think to myself that I am the only kid that is not in school besides Billy Bob. He's hurt. I go to see the little old ladies. They need me to shop, and stay and play.

As I walk to the store, I see Reverend Jones. He has two kids atop one of his big Great Danes. They're having lots of fun. I want to ride also, but I must get back to the ladies, and help them as much as I can. They need me. Somehow, the ladies find out that the big kid next door and I are over at the store late at night. They tell me to stop, and I say that I will. They make a few hot dogs as I drink soda pop. We talk of how we miss the other ladies and all the funny things they once talked about. I tell the ladies that I am going to go and visit my pal Billy Bob in the morning. The ladies said they would pray for him and wished him well.

The next day, Billy Bob's dad comes to pick me up. He's glad to see me, and says I'm growing tall. We get to the ranch, and Rex and his parents are there, also. Billy Bob is sitting in a recliner under the shade tree, next to the barn and horse pen with his mother. He sees me and tries to sit up, but his mother says to him, "Easy, baby cowboy." Billy Bob is so happy to see me and I'm excited to see my pal, also. He has a cast on his leg, and a cast on his arm. His left baby finger is broken, also. He said he wasn't in much pain. The first report of him having broken ribs is not true. He's banged up and sore, but his ribs are fine. *Great news*, I thought. He jokes with me about not being in school this year, and says that he and I must be the only kids in town not going to school. I said "Yes, you're right, but you will be back soon, Billy Bob. Hurry and get well, my friend." He tells Rex and me that his mother is going to sell the rest of the horses. "Say it ain't so, boys! Say it ain't so!" I yelled. "Cellulose John Wayne Jay," Rex said to me, "We are still going to be able to ride at my house. No one is selling my horses." It's getting late, and so they take me back home. *What a blessed day. My pals are fine, and we will get together again soon.*

I must play my guitar tonight for my aunt. My daddy's new wife taught us lots of songs. I am going to sing one tonight. My sisters are not here to back-ground sing for me, but my guitar can sing. *Jesus Loves Me, Yes I Know*, is the song I have selected. My aunt is sitting by the piano, with happy eyes. I start to play and sing, and she starts to cry. She didn't know I was that good. She had heard me making noise before, but not real music, like now. She joins me with the piano, and we sound like something great. She is so proud of me and cannot understand how I learned so fast.

The next day I get my canteen, my rope, and carrots, and go on another adventure. Off I go, back through the Hobo Trail, across the creek and over the bridge, down the train tracks for a five-mile-walk to find those horses that the kid next door told me about. This is my second trip out here. I hope they still live here- it's been awhile. I walk around, but see no horses, so I climb a tree almost to the top. Lo and behold, there is a large herd over the hill! I'm so excited that I almost fall out of the tree. I only saw a few head before. I didn't bring enough carrots for all these horses. I see a man coming down the trail on horseback. He is inside with the horses, and looks like he is going to ride a few. I sit in the tree for hours watching the cowboy ride about four horses. Now I can see that some are not wild. He's got about twenty-one head of horses. All I need is one. Next time, I hope to ride. As I walk back home, I see more horses to my right. They're the ones that did not get a carrot during my last trip. There are three horses, and I have three carrots in my back pocket. I go under the fence and they come to me. I give each of them a carrot, and pet them on the head. *I hope I can ride you one day.* I start the long walk home. *Thank you, Lord. Oh Lord, what a blessed day in the life of a stick horse baby cowboy.*

When I reached home, my aunt met me at the door to tell me the white cub scouts are accepting black kids at this time. She asked if I would like to join. I am already a scout- a pony scout. Very soon I fall asleep thinking of a pony, when the big kid next door taps on my window. I tell him I can't go tonight. He says maybe next time. I fall back to sleep. I am up early the next morning. I will walk to school with all the kids from the circle and then I'll go across the street to see Cleopatra and my baby sister. My big sister is already in class. She loves school so much that she gets there early.

My mother is going to have a baby soon, and I hope it's a boy. Some of the big boys from the circle are running very fast by the house on their way to high school. They tell me that one day I'll be a big boy scout- going to meetings three nights a week. As time passes the big boys would show me their uniforms and all of their camping gear, and would sometimes camp out next door at the big kid's house. Then I would go over and learn things the little scouts do and things the big scouts do. I'm only six, and I think I like horses better than boy scouts. *Maybe later,* I thought. (Six years later, I found out that you have to be twelve-years-old to be a big boy scout. I've got lots of horses to scout, and to ride).

Elvis is back at the movies, and everyone is going. This time, I make sure it's not showing at the all-White movie house like before, when I wasn't allowed in. I see my pal from next door and he tells me Elvis will be showing at the mixed movie house, and he has a ticket for me. What a pal! He likes girls now, and I can't get him to go pony scouting or riding with me. He still lets me know where to find the horses that are not too far from the house.

Rex and his father are coming to get me today. They want me to camp out at the ranch this weekend. My aunt says it's okay. I'm going to the Elvis show at noon and then to the ranch at four o'clock. *Thank you, Lord.* I go and play my guitar a bit before the big Elvis show.

Excitement fills my body as the movie starts. Lots of people are here today. The place is packed. Blacks are on the top floor, and Whites are on the bottom floor. No one throws popcorn today- everyone is just happy to see Elvis, at last. What a show!

I run down the train tracks across the creek, over the bridge, and through the Hobo Trail. I'm home now. I pack a few things and before I know it, my friend, Rex, and his mother and father are here. They get out of the car. They want to talk to my aunt. They go inside. Rex and I sit on the steps out front. Soon, they say, "Let's ride, baby cowboys!" We stopped for ice cream and they wanted to hear about the Elvis movie. I told them that I had a great time, and would love to see the next Elvis movie that comes to town. I told them how much I'd like to see Billy Bob, and hope he can walk again soon. Lo and behold, I see Billy Bob's daddy's truck. And there is my friend, sitting in a chair with a big smile on his face. It's Billy Bob's birthday! What a surprise! The kid can walk a little bit. "Easy, baby cowboy!" his daddy yelled. We are so glad to see one another. It's been awhile. We three boys are going to sleep in the barn with the horses tonight. Billy Bob can walk, with the help of crutches. The parents bring dinner. After we eat, the baby cowboy gets a cake. They say to make a wish and blow out the candles. "I made the wish last week," he said to us all, "and my wish came true. I just wanted to see my pals. And now, here we are, all together again." Then, he blows out the candles. We have cake, and more ice cream. What a great day! After the grown ups say good night, we boys stay up talking half of the night, until we fall asleep.

The next morning when the boys get up, I'm in the pen next to the barn, riding a pony. They call for me, and we talk of what the day may bring for us. "Let's feed the stock, go inside, get cleaned up and eat a little bit, then go from there." Billy Bob can't ride yet, but Rex has a cart and a pony to pull it. We put Billy Bob in the cart and saddle up our horses and head out through the field, down by the pond and over the grass hills. What a big ranch! We baby cowboys play around half the day before the fathers ride out in the truck to bring lunch, and to check on the cows. My pals and I have lost track of time. I tell my pals that my mother is going to have a baby and they tell me one of the horses in the barn where we camped out is going to have a baby, also. *How thrilling*! I've seen a baby before- my baby sister, Francine. "Boys, I want to see that baby pony when he's born!" They said it would be awhile, but that they would come and get me when the time comes. "And I'll make sure you boys see my new baby sister or brother when that time comes." Rex and I helped Billy Bob down from the cart, and then carefully sat him down on a big log. We began to eat and make plans. We decided to go for a swim. Billy Bob can't swim, but he can put his feet in the water. We put him at the pond's edge, then Rex and I jumped in. The water is not very deep. We can stand up in it. Billy Bob tells us that he may be going back to school in two weeks. That's great news. We are so happy that our little pal didn't die when he fell from his pony. The kid was once in bad shape, but he's back now. *Thank you, Lord.* Oh, how time flies when you're having fun!

The next day, Billy Bob goes to the doctor to get checked out. His mother thinks the cast on his leg is about to fall off. Maybe he can go to school sooner than expected. Rex and I go on a tour while Billy Bob is away. We ride next door to the black kid's house and play a bit. He's a big boy like Rex. They go to the same school but are not classmates. The new kid is in third grade. We say goodbye, get on our horses and ride away down the side of the road. All we see ahead is time and space- lots of space. There is not a car or truck in sight. Another road, to the right, is where Rex would like to ride, but it's getting late so we turn around. When we get back to the barn, the fathers are inside with the newborn pony, and he is drinking his mother's milk. "What a nice looking pony!" I said. He has only been in the world a few hours. What a blessed day. Rex and I will give our horses a much needed bath.

After awhile, Billy Bob is back from the doctor's office. He is going to be just fine. The cast is off of his leg, but still on his arm. He can walk much better than before. We eat and talk of riding through the little country town tomorrow. The fathers said we can take the back road- no one takes that road much anymore. They have a new road now that takes you to the big city and most people use that road. We plan to get a good night's sleep. It's going to be about a five-mile-ride roundtrip for us baby cowboys. We are very excited! The boys' parents come out to the barn to check on us, and the newborn pony. They tell me that my aunt is on the phone and she wants to talk to me. The parents all have happy eyes as I walk past them to the ranch house. I get to the phone, and my aunt tells me that Cleopatra has a new baby and I have a brand new baby brother. What a happy day! "I'll be home tomorrow," I say to my aunt. I tell her about the great time we are having. She is happy for me, and she also tells me that she and I may take a trip to Texas next week to visit her sister. I run back to the barn with happy eyes and a happy heart. I tell the boys about my little brother. They are thrilled for me. It's getting late, so we try and get some sleep after the boys' parents go inside the house- but we find ourselves talking for most of the night.

Morning comes fast. I'm up feeding horses when the boys get up from their sleeping bags. We all go inside and get cleaned up. We eat, and then off we go. We saddle up three horses. Billy Bob is going to ride; no cart for him today. The cast is off, and his leg feels great. It looks like rain's coming but we don't care. I think to myself that it was raining when my pal fell off his horse months ago. We will ride until the rain starts, then we will turn back toward the barn. We want to take Billy Bob on a tour. As we ride the back road, we are greeted by two boys we've never seen before. "We have horses, too," the boys said to us. "We live up the road, if you cowboys want to come visit." Billy Bob, Rex and I said, "Sure, how far up the road?" The boys are riding their bikes, and said to follow them. It's only about a mile. It looks like the rain is moving away from us. When we get to the new kids' house, we see lots of cows, dogs, chickens, pigs, goats and horses. I've never seen this many animals before. We are having a great time! The new kids go to the same school as Rex. They are older boys, and have ten horses on the farm. After giving us a tour of the place, we meet the parents. The mother makes lunch for us, and tells us not to be out late. Her kids are going to the drive-in movie tonight. They saddle two horses and we ride around the farm. *What a nice place to live!* As we lose

28

track of time, we see Rex and Billy Bob's fathers driving up the road. They are looking for us. We have to turn back. Billy Bob's daddy has to leave town with his job. We say goodbye to our new pals, "Until we meet again. Peace."

When we get home, Rex and Billy Bob's mothers are out front with the new baby pony. He is running around the yard, playing with his mother. We give our horses a bath, then we brush, water, and feed them. What a great weekend! It's like camping with the Boy Scouts- only on horseback. What a great adventure. We pack up, and in the car we go. We say goodbye to Rex and his parents, and thanked them for their hospitality. Billy Bob and his parents drop me off at my aunt's house. We say goodbye, and I thank them for a great weekend. I run from the car, up the stairs, and into my aunt's waiting arms. She is very happy to see me. I have never been away from her for so long. I missed her. She tells me to take a bath and get dressed. "I'm taking you home to see your new baby brother." While my aunt is getting dressed, I run down the street to see the sweet little old ladies. I missed them, and they missed me, as well. A cowboy update is what they want, and that is what they get. I tell them, "I have to go to Cleo's house, but I'll be back tomorrow to talk more story." "Sure, baby cowboy," they say to me. I rush back home.

My aunt and I walk ten blocks to my mother's house. My sisters are sitting out front playing with their dolls. I'm so glad to see them. I go inside. I kiss my mother and she tells me that the baby is sleeping. We go in his room. What a big baby he is! He's the second new baby I've ever seen. *What a blessed day*, I thought. *Thank you, Lord.* I have a little brother. His name is Deano. I'm sure he's a baby cowboy, and I'm going to take him with me on some of my adventures.

The next day, I work for the ladies and help my aunt around the house. I play my guitars and the piano. When the phone rings, it's my daddy- the Guitar Man, Abner Wingate Jay. We talk for awhile, and he asks about my sisters and Cleopatra. They don't have a phone. I tell him that I have a new baby brother. He wishes us well, and then I play him a song over the phone with one of my three guitars. He is thrilled that I have progressed so quickly. We say goodbye, and Abner wants to talk to my aunt. Before I pass the phone to my aunt, my daddy tells me to stay alert and pay attention when I'm around ponies. "Sure thing."

The next day, I ride my bike across and behind the shopping center, down the Hobo Trail, across the creek and over the bridge to the train tracks. Off I go- pony scouting- and I've got to get some carrots. I stop at the country store about a mile from the horses that I'm hoping to ride. The last time I was here, I saw a cowboy to the right, up the hill, riding some horses- the black, the white, the paint and the gold pony. Those are good horses to start with. I watched him ride, from atop a tree, and they didn't look wild to me. I'm sure I can ride, if no one is around. I'm glad I bought a whole bag of carrots this time, because as soon as I put my bike in the bushes and walk a bit, I see horses- lots more than before! I slapped my face, just to make sure I wasn't dreaming! There were so many, that I couldn't count them all right away. Later, I counted twenty-two horses of all colors and sizes. What a thrill! I think I will call this little piece of heaven, "Baby Cowboy Hill." The wonderful horses I saw the man riding are out too far in the middle of the pasture for me to try and catch. I fear being caught, or busted, by the owner. Let's face it, I am trespassing, which is against the law- even for baby cowboys such as myself. So I take a chance with a bay-looking pony that is very close to me. I'm sure I can catch him. He is walking in the trees when I give him a carrot. I slide my string rope around his neck, and walk with him deeper into the forest where I tie him to a tree branch. I began to rub the pony all over his body- as much as I could reach. I did not have a comb or brush. "My hands will just have to do," I said to the pony. He bent his head up and down, as if he was happy, and wanted another carrot. *I have two more left. I must save some for the horses down the track, heading toward home.* I move the pony close to a log about two feet away. I get on the log, grab a handful of hair from his neck, and jump onto his back. We ride slow and easy through the lush, cool forest. No one is around, and I stay far away from the rest of the horses. I hear the sound of water. I look ahead and see a creek. I want to cross it, but the pony won't go. I don't think he has ever crossed this creek. So we turn around and head for my bike. I hear the sound of kids playing. I ride to the fence, close to my bike. When I jump from the pony, I give him a big treat- one remaining carrot. He loves carrots. I pet him, and off I go, over to my bike.

I have a bag of carrots for the other horses down the track. I see kids walking far ahead of me. I slow down, so as not to be noticed, because I want to check and see if I can find the other horses. I go off the train track and put my bike in the bushes and jump the fence. The horses were here under the trees the last time I visited, but I see nothing at this point, so I keep walking slow and easy down the trail. I look to my left, and see hoof tracks. After walking a bit, I stop and climb up a tree for a better view. Boy, what a view! There is a big lake, and seven horses over the hill. What a wonderful sight to see! I rest in the tree, and eat the small carrot in my pocket, as I drink from my canteen. It's getting late, and I feel today is not a good day to try these horses. I need a closer look, but I don't have time to walk over the hill down by the lake. I don't know the owners of these horses, and they are not going to be happy to see me trespassing on this land. So I ease my way down the tree, to the ground, and walk back to my bike. Off I go, down the track toward home. It's going to be my job, to ride these bottom horses first, the next time I'm here. I'm almost home, as

I pass the kids from down the train track. We say hello, but we don't stop. As I ride, I wonder if those are the kids who own the horses.

When I reach home, I kiss my aunt and get cleaned up. I should eat, but I'm too excited. I tell my aunt of my adventure and of the new land, the big lake, and the wonderful horses I saw. It was a very good day.

I'm in my room playing my guitar, and my aunt comes in to tell me that we might go to Texas in the morning. She tells me that her sister is not feeling well. Morning comes fast. I'm up, and off to my mother's house I go. I'm not sure how long I'll be gone, so I want to see my family before I go. My little baby brother is a very happy boy. I can't wait until he grows up. He just may be a cowboy. My sisters would like me to bring them a new doll. Cleopatra wants me to pay attention and to stay alert. I kissed the girls, the baby, and my mama. "Goodbye, until we meet again. I am going to Texas." I rush ten blocks to get back home. I go past my aunt's house to the little old ladies' house. No one is sitting out front, so I go up to the door, and the door opens. "Good morning!" I said to the sweet little old lady. "Good morning, baby cowboy." "I'm going to Texas today and I want to let all of you ladies know. I don't have time to go around the circle to the other ladies' houses, so would you please let the girls know?" "Yes, I will, sonny boy" she replied. "Come here, kid, let me kiss you, because I don't know when I will see you again. I miss you already! Be good, and hurry back to us girls." "Yes ma'am." And off I go, down the street.

My aunt is on the phone calling a cab to take us to the bus station. "How far is Texas?" I asked my aunt. "A long way, John Wayne. We will be in Texas tomorrow." When we get to the bus station and get checked in, I ask my aunt to give me the phone numbers to Rex and Billy Bob's houses. I know they are in school, but maybe someone is home. I call Rex and his mother picks up the phone. She is happy to hear from me. I tell her to tell the baby cowboys that I have gone to Texas, and I don't know when I'll be back. She tells me to take care of myself and to hurry back home soon. She knows that her boy Rex, and his pal Billy Bob, are going to miss me. They love me, and I love them as well. I'm the first black kid they've ever met in their lives, and they are the first two white boys I've ever met. I can't swim in the White public pool or join the country club or go in some stores downtown without my parents, but that's how it is for now. I'm so glad my pals and their parents are good and righteous people. *Thank you, Lord.*

My aunt calls to me. The bus is ready, and off to Texas we go. I'm going on another adventure. I'm sure I'll see Mustang horses everywhere- it's Texas- big country with lots of wild horses. Maybe my uncle will take me down to the big ranch. I feel myself falling to sleep. I try and fight it, but I can't. I'm dreaming of horses and cows and Elvis. I'm still thinking about the Elvis show. I awake after a few hours. There are horses on both sides of the road. What a wonderful sight to see! There is a kid in the back of the bus, and I go talk to him. He say's his name is Dan, and that he and his mother are going to California. He's in the second grade. We talk and eat lunch together. The bus stops, and we have to change buses. I tell Dan goodbye. My aunt and I go to the next bus. The bus starts rolling off to Texas. There are lots of people on this bus, but I'm able to get the back seat, so I can sleep. I think of the little old ladies and wonder who will go to the store for them while I'm away. The poor ladies are all gone to heaven, except for three of them. Oh, how I miss them- dead or alive. They didn't even get a real cowboy update before I left. I'll have lots to tell them when I get back.

After a few hours, the bus makes another stop. I try to sleep, but there is too much excitement all around for me to sleep. My aunt tells me it won't be long now, as we cross the Texas line. We have one more bus to catch. We go inside to eat. We have only a short time before the bus is ready. A lot of big kids are in the station. I find out that they are on a school field trip. My aunt calls out to me that the bus is ready, and off we go again. By the time we get to my aunt's house, I'm asleep. I don't wake up until the next day.

I sit up in the bed and look around. I have been here before, but it's been awhile. This is a very big house. I go downstairs, calling to my aunts. They yell to me that they are out in the backyard. I find my way through the big house, and hug and kiss my aunts. We sit and talk for hours, until my uncle comes home from work. He is happy to see me. How glad I am to see him, too. He gets cleaned up, and we eat. They show me the rest of the house. My uncle tells me that maybe his son will have time to take me to my first Texas ranch and farm. I'm getting ready for a big day tomorrow. I want to ride my first Texas pony.

I fall asleep very easily, and morning comes fast. I'm the first one up. I take a bath and get dressed, and down the stairs I go. My uncle is up now, and I smell something cooking. "Good morning, sir," I say. "Good morning, John Wayne. Would you like to eat?" "Yes, sir." "I hope you had a good night's sleep, John Wayne, because I'm taking you to work with me today." As my uncle is getting dressed, I hurry and eat. My aunts are awake and calling for me. I hug and kiss them both. They tell me to be a good boy, and off we go. My uncle and I head downtown to work. "What do you do at your work?" I ask. "Tailoring, my boy; custom made garments and dry cleaning is what we do." We pull in front of a big shop. We get out and go inside. There are garments hanging from the top to the bottom of the shop. It is very hot, and steam is all over the place. There are lots of big blow fans everywhere. My uncle takes me on a tour of the place, and I meet the people who work in the back- where all the action is. I'm just a kid, and the action is too hot for me. "A little bit at a time," my uncle tells me. "It takes awhile to get used to the heat. I need you to go down the street, to the store on the corner, and pick up garments from the shopkeeper. And get yourself a soda pop. Be careful, and watch out for the cars." He gives me one dollar as I walk outside. I'm excited about being in the Lone Star state of Texas.

Although I saw lots of horses on the roads coming here, I cannot wait to get my hands on a Texas pony. I walk about five blocks and go inside the store. I pick up the garments and then I get a soda pop. The man wants to know if I'm sure that I can return the garments in three days. "Yes, sir. I'm sure, but you can call the shop to be really sure. Goodbye." I rush back to the shop and my uncle is happy to see me. He needs me to help clean up the place. He tells me that his son is coming after lunch to meet me, and take me to the farm. I smell adventure, and I'm ready.

The morning is moving by fast. A cab pulls up out front and my aunts have arrived. They have just come from the doctor's office, and they say they are feeling fine. They will work in the shop the rest of the day. I finish cleaning, and then my aunt wants me to go to the store. It's a few blocks up the street. They write a note for me to give the shopkeeper. I get the items and rush back to the dry cleaning shop. When I get back, my uncle calls for me. His son is here to get me. We say hello, and off we go. We ride for about an hour, and I see lots of horses and cows. When we get to the gate of the ranch, two dogs meet us. My cousin owns big Texas Long horn cows. I've never seen cows like this before. I see a pony that I would like to ride. He tells me that the pony is green broke. "What is green broke?" I ask. "He needs more training," my cousin says to me. "How about that black and white spot pony?" "Sure," I answered. We get the saddle from the truck. My cousin will ride his old mare bareback. We put more water into our canteens, for it's a very, very hot day. My cousin says we will ride down the road through the trees, and up the hill to the pond. He asks me if I can swim. I tell him I can swim only if the water is not deep. I have only been in the water a few times, and I could stand up in it. If I can't touch the bottom, I'm not sure how long I could stay afloat. I need a real swimming lesson.

We stop, and get off of the horses. We sit and have a snack, and drink from our canteens near a small creek bed. There is not much water, but enough to let the horses have a drink. He tells me when they finish, that he has to ride fast over the hill to look for the Long horn cows. He tells me to tie my pony to a tree, then to sit and take a nap. He says he won't be long. I sit and lean back against a tree, across from my pony. I think about the little old ladies, my mother, sisters and little baby brother. I hope all is well with my pals, Rex and Billy Bob. I'll be in school very soon. I can already read and write and count. I feel myself falling asleep. After an hour or so, my cousin comes back, herding a few Long horn cows. He is going to put them in another pasture. He tells me to run and open the gate. He tells me that it's about time I learn about Longhorns- but not today- it's getting late. We ride back to the truck and unsaddle the horses. He has no barn, so we turn them out. They run fast up the hill to the pond. What a wonderful sight! We get in the truck and off we go, down the long dirt road to the main gate. My cousin gets out to open the gate, then drives through and I get out to close and lock the gate. *What a blessed day. Thank you, Lord.* My cousin says that he will ride the green broke pony I like, so that I can ride it the next time I'm out here. I jump back in the truck and off we go, back to town. I fall asleep as we make the long trip. When we arrive back home, my cousin has to go to work, so we say goodbye.

I run inside and they all want a cowboy update. What an adventure! We talk for hours until dinner time. My uncle and his wife will be going to the shop tomorrow. My aunt and I will stay home and rest. We all say good night. I fall asleep thinking of a pony. When I wake up, my aunt surprises me- my guitar is in the bed next to me. She sent it the day before we left home. She wants me to play for her, and tells me I'm getting better. She wants me to play for my aunt and uncle tonight. I go get cleaned up, dressed, and eat, then I'm out the door. I want to walk around and check things out. There are lots of kids down the street. I think I'll go say hello.

Some kids are playing baseball and they ask me if I want to play. I said I did, but I didn't know the game very well. They said they would show me how to play. We play awhile, when two of the boys stop, and say they have to go home. So, I stop also. I find out that the boys live next door to me, so we walk home together. We talk of school, and I learn that this will be their first year, also. They are very excited. The school the boys will attend is right on our block. They want to take me over to the playground tomorrow. We say goodnight.

I go inside and my aunt tells me, with sad eyes, that two of the sweet little old ladies have passed on to heaven. How sad. How very sad. Those little old ladies and I spent a lot of wonderful days together. Bless them all. And may they rest in peace. Those girls always put a smile on my face. Just thinking about them makes me cry. They would always tell me to stay alert and pay attention. I'm going to miss the ladies who have gone to cowgirl heaven, and the one lone cowgirl that's left. I can't wait to get home and see her. All of her girlfriends have gone to greener pastures. She is all alone- until I get back there- when every evening I will do what I can for her. She would love a cowboy update right about now, I'm sure. My aunt tells me later that the lone cowgirl's kids are coming to visit her very soon, and maybe she will go back to their home in Mississippi. She is getting old and weak, and needs someone to look after her. I'm getting sleepy and I feel very sad. I say goodnight, and up the stairs I go. I try to play my guitar, but I'm just not feeling it. So I fall asleep slowly, while thinking of the old white hobo man, on the Hobo Trail behind the horse pen, who helped me over the fence, and then caught the big white horse for me to ride. I also think of his pal who had too much to drink, and how he lay in the grass, sleeping it off. The little old lady cowgirls had told me what to do with the pony. I'm sure glad the Hobo and his pal were sitting around the trail that day to help me. *Thank you, Lord.* I awake in the middle of the night, crying, and I can't stop. I go down the hallway and get in bed with my aunt. She tells me that the girls have gone home, to God in heaven, and they are in a much better place. "They are at peace, John Wayne. God doesn't make mistakes. We are all very sad, but life goes on. We live and we die. Now go to sleep, baby cowboy, and dream of catching a wild Texas Mustang. I'll see you in the morning, baby." So I fall back to sleep, but not in my bed.

Morning comes fast. I get up and run down the hallway to my room. I change and get ready to go to the shop with my uncle. I go downstairs to eat with him, and we talk about life and death. Among other things, he wants to hear me play my guitar. He tells me I can take it to work with us. When we get to the shop, I have to deliver garments around the block for my uncle. It's not so hot today. Maybe I can go and explore, deeper into town. First, I must get back and find out my other duties. I see lots of people out walking this morning. After I drop off the garments, I rush back and my uncle wants me to sweep out the place. He also wants me to clean the windows that I am able to reach. When I finish, my aunts come in to work. They both have happy eyes. They hug and kiss me. I love them so. After I finished the windows, doors and floors, I get my guitar from out back in my uncle's car. I start to play, and everyone stops to listen. They look on with happy eyes. My aunt and uncle are very impressed. They think that someday, I could be as good as my daddy, Abner Wingate Jay.

Now the ladies are getting ready to call the fried chicken house and order some lunch. I will have to go down and pick it up. It's about a five-block-walk. As I'm walking down the street, I see my cousin driving up the road near the back of the shop. He yells for me to come over to him. When I cross the road, he takes a kid's saddle from the truck bed. He tells me that the saddle is for me. "Thank you!" I yell. "In a few days I should have your new pony trained. We've got Texas Long horn cattle to round up for the market," he tells me. How excited I am! I'd better rush down and get lunch before I forget. I'm in cowboy mode. I've got nothing but ponies on my mind. I get back to the shop with the fried chicken lunches, but I'm too excited to eat. My uncle says I can go down the street to play with the new kids that I met earlier.

The kids are playing basketball, but I'm too little to play with the big boys. I don't know the game very well, but it looks fun. As I start my walk back to the shop, I see kids my age coming down the sidewalk. They have books. They must be coming from school. I stop and talk to them for awhile. The boy is in second grade, and his sister is in the first grade. "Can I see your book?" I asked. "Sure." So we sat on the corner, down by the shop. When I opened the book, I saw horses. It's a storybook about a pony named Blackie. I asked them if they would read the story to me. They told me that they are not good readers yet. "I can read," I tell them. The story is about a wild black horse that no one can catch. All the cowboys in town have been trying to put a rope on him for years. No one has yet.

My aunt is standing out in front of the shop. She calls for me and the kids to come and finish the rest of the chicken lunch and soda pop. The kids want to know how I can read so well when I'm not even in school yet. I say to them that my aunt taught me to read, write and count. She was once a teacher. "Hello, kids," my aunt says. We sit on the steps in front of the shop, eating and reading. The kids have to get back home. They tell me where they live, and say I can come play anytime. It's only two blocks behind the shop. My aunts and uncle have to work late today. They tell me that I can go home and play with the kids next door.

As I'm walking home, I stop in at The Cut. The Cut is where teenagers hang out after school. They eat ice cream and burgers, and drink soda pop, and music is everywhere. I stop and get ice cream. I talk to some of the big kids. I ask them how they like school. They like it. They want to know what school I attend. "I'm just a kid and I don't go to school yet, but I will very soon." "You're going to love school, kid," one of the girls said to me. When I get home, my cowboy cousin is putting my new saddle in my room. He has to go and work now and says that he and I will talk later. My aunt and uncle are home, and want me to say hello to my little girl cousin, Peach. She is very nice and already goes to school. She saw my saddle and guitar in my room, and wants to hear me play. She loves music. I play *The Lord Loves Me, This I Know*. Peach has very happy eyes at the sound of my guitar. She knows the song, and sings along with me as I play. We laugh and play until late. She has to go to school early, so we say goodnight to one another. I go downstairs and my uncle is already asleep, but my aunts are still talking. They hug and kiss me, and tell me to go to bed. "You are going to ride a Texas mustang tomorrow," they say.

The night goes by so fast that I don't even have time to dream about a pony. I hear foot steps. It's my cowboy cousin, and he is in my room getting my saddle. "Get up, kid, we've got cows to move. I'm going to cook us breakfast while you get ready." Off we go. As we drive, he tells me that I can ride the mustang today. He's still green, but not as green as before. We stop on the way to the ranch and pick up a man who my cousin called, "Cowboy." He will help us today. "Hey, baby cowboy!" he says to me. "Hello, Mr. Cowboy!" I answer. As we ride, they talk of their plans for today. I see lots of horses and cows on both sides of the road. I'm in Texas, and there are big trucks everywhere with horses and cows inside. We stop at the gate. Mr. Cowboy gets out and opens the gate as we drive in, then closes the gate behind us. We go down the long dirt road to catch the horses. We see them off to the left, and we stop. The horses walk slowly to the truck. I count seven, but I don't see the mustang. We catch and saddle three horses, and ride up the hill. Soon we see the rest of the horses and lots of cows. All alone by the creek, under the trees, I see the Texas mustang. I ride over, put a rope over his head, and then lead the pony down to where the cowboys are. My cousin takes his saddle, puts it on the mustang and rides him around awhile. Then, I take my saddle off the horse that I'm riding, and turn him loose. Then I put my new saddle on the Texas mustang. After awhile, we go scouting for cattle. We see a few up the road. As we get closer, my cousin says they are not the ones that he wants. So we push on, up and over the next hill. What a wonderful adventure this is for a baby cowboy! It just now hit me- real hard- that I am in the Lone Star state of Texas, I've got a new saddle on a very nice Texas mustang pony, and I see big Texas Long horns all around me. As I think back to the morning in Ohio when I jumped from my grandmother's window on the second-floor, seeking to catch a black and white pony, I can say, "Thank you Lord, for not letting me break my little cowboy neck!"

The cowboys find the cattle they like. They tell me to stay back, and when they turn the herd around I can join them, bringing up the rear. This Texas mustang wants to run. He is tough to handle for a baby cowboy. I remember what the sweet little old lady cowgirls told me. "Turn him in a circle, John Wayne, and talk him down easy." I would always ask the cowgirls what to do if this or that happens. They always had something to say, or a story of when they were baby cowgirls, and of the tough horses they rode. I miss them and I feel tears forming in my eyes. This is not the time for cries or goodbyes- I've got to pay attention and stay alert. I've got a Texas mustang to ride. If he runs, we could start a real stampede. That spells trouble. The cows are moving easy, and we are pushing about twenty-five head. I stay well back, like the boys told me to. My pony has calmed down a lot. He's just feeling good. What a blessed day in the life of a baby cowboy! When we get near the dirt road, we look down the hill and the trucks are here. We push the cattle, slow and easy down to the stock pens, and into the trucks. We have more to round up, but not today. Next week we'll be ready to round up, and push them in the stock pens once again. After the cows are gone, we unsaddle the horses. While I hose down the ponies, the cowboys drink a beer. I guess that's what cowboys do after the job is done. I'm just a baby cowboy, and I want a drink of water.

While the horses are tied up and drying in the sun, I go to the truck to find a soft brush. When the horses dry, I brush them all over, and then I turn them loose and watch as they run to the top of the hill. I think they are happy to be free.

Through the gate, and off we go, to drop the cowboy off at his house. He has four nice looking horses in his front yard. He says I can ride them anytime I want. "Thank you, sir," I say as we drive off. My cousin drops me off in front of the house and I get my saddle from the truck bed. I say goodnight to him and he thanks me, and tells me that I did a very good job today. I go inside, and a cowboy update is what the family wants. They can see adventure in my eyes. We stay up past ten o'clock talking about the wonderful day on a Texas ranch. I told them of the Texas mustang, lots of horses, and the pride of the Lone Star State- Texas Long horn cattle. What a day in the life a of a baby cowboy. *Thank you, Lord.* My little cousin, Peach, wants to know more, but my aunts tell us to get some sleep.

I can't fall asleep because I'm thinking of the sweet little old ladies in the circle. There is only one cowgirl left. I hope she's home and well when I get back. I miss all of the cowgirls very much. I feel myself falling slowly off to sleep as I think of all the horses I'm going to ride before I get to cowboy heaven.

The next day comes fast. I'm up early and it's still dark outside. I love the dark. I go out and sit on the front steps. No one is around. There is not a car on the street. I hear chickens and I hear dogs barking. I miss my mother, sisters and baby brother. I miss my pals Rex and Billy Bob. I'll see those baby cowboys real soon. We have lots of cowboy updates to share. The lights are on in the house. It must be my uncle- he's going to eat soon. I go in, and get cleaned up and dressed. Then I eat with my uncle. It's five o'clock in the morning, and off to work my uncle and I go. We stop on the way to pick up garments to take to the shop for same-day cleaning. He tells me that I'll have more pick-ups later. I go in and sweep the place out and take out the trash. I take care of the flowers and give them water. I go outside and pull weeds along the side of the shop. I'm going to make a trip to the store for my uncle. I see kids walking to school. I'm thinking that I'll be going to school real soon. I get the items from the store, and back to the shop I go. When I get there, my uncle tells me that his son's pal, the cowboy, is going to come by and get me to ride horses at his ranch. The last time I saw the cowboy, rounding up, he said he would let me ride some of his horses. I now see that he is a man of his word. I smell adventure in the air, and my uncle says he will be here in two hours. I'll have to hurry and make two pick-ups before he comes for me. In the meantime, my aunts are out front talking to some lady friend. I'm looking out the window, and see that my aunts have bags of garments. I go out and bring them inside. They introduce me to the lady. She is having a party over the weekend for her grandkids, and she wants Peach and me to come to her party. "Thank you, ma'am, I'd love to." The cowboy is here now, and he has his teenage son with him. They talk to my aunts, then go inside to talk with my uncle. The plan for today, according to the cowboy, is to break two very wild Texas mustangs. "The baby cowboy will not be near the wild horses. He will be outside, looking in, while my son and I do the work," the cowboy assures my aunt and uncle. "Don't worry about the kid. He's in good hands with us. See you later," and off we go.

Their spread is just a short ride from town. It's a very swell place to be. They get a pony for me to ride. I clean the pony up and saddle him, and ride around in the pen. The cowboy and his son are going out back to get their mustangs. Whey they return, they run the wild horses into the pen next to where I'm riding. My first wild horses- what a wonderful sight! They are jumping around, kicking and bucking all over the place. They put a rope on one of the mustangs and saddle him. He runs around and around with excitement. The cowboy's teenage son jumps on the pony, and off they go, bucking, running and kicking high in the air. I don't think he likes that saddle. The kid's off, bucked into the fence and he's on the ground. His daddy gets in the pen to check the kid out, and he's fine. Then the cowboy jumps on the pony. Same action for daddy- bucking and kicking, around and around they go, until the pony calms down slowly. He is walking now instead of running. The cowboy gets off, and puts the kid back on the mustang. He rides around for awhile, until the daddy opens the main gate. "Let him out, kid!" he yelled to his son. And they jet out of the pen moving very hard and fast, and full of wild horse action. Cowboy says they will ride the pony to the lake down the road. The water is not deep at the edge. The pony walks easy like, and soon the cowboy stops and sits for awhile, and talks to the pony. They began to make small circles, deeper into the water until the water is almost up to the mustang's mouth. The pony is going for a swim, and he looks as if he's having fun. After a short while, he brings the pony up on the bank and ties him to a tree. His son goes to get the other mustang in the pen, and brings it down by the lake. Cowboy jumps back on the mustang, and leads the other pony around as he goes back into the water, pulling the pony beside him. The pony follows, and it looks like he loves the lake. After a few circles, they come up on the bank. Then we all ride back to the ranch. Cowboy and his son will ride the other mustang tomorrow. The son will hose down the horses and brush them out while his father takes me to town. I say goodbye to the kid and he tells me I did a good job. "Thanks, cowboy. See you," and off we go.

The cowboy and I stop at The Cut. We order milk shakes and fries. We sit in the parking lot and eat, while the cowboy talks of the pony days long ago, and of the wild horses he and his dad rode. His dad worked at a machine shop on a big Texas horse and cattle ranch. Before and after work, the boss would let him ride the wild horses. Soon, he became very good at it. After a broken arm, and a banged-up knee, I'd say he's ahead in the game- if we're keeping score. He tells me that he's been on over one hundred wild horses in his spare time, starting long before his teenage son was born. We finish eating, and off to my house we go. It's just down the street. I thank the cowboy for the wonderful day we shared. "Any time," he said. I stand in front of the house watching as he drives out of sight, saying to myself, *What a cowboy, and what a man. Thank you Lord. I have met three Texas wild horse wranglers and seen lots of horses. I've seen the pride of the Lone Star State- many big Texas Longhorns, and I rode a green broke, wonderful little mustang pony. What a blessed day, looking through the eyes of a baby cowboy.*

I have ice cream for my little girl cousin. It's about to melt so I rush to the kitchen to keep from making a mess. I put the ice cream in the icebox. No one is home, so I go upstairs to my room and get cleaned up. Soon, everyone arrives home. I let Peach know about her ice cream and I have not forgotten about the cowboy update. I say hello to my aunts and uncles. They are tired from working hard all day, and retire early to their rooms. Peach and I stay up long into the night talking of my baby cowboy adventures. There is no school tomorrow and we are going to a party. There will be cake and ice cream, lots of kids, and lots of music. My uncle's son, the cowboy, is walking inside the house. He just finished work and wants to know how things went today on his friend's ranch. I tell him that his friend told me that he will pick me up the day after tomorrow. We still have Texas Longhorns to round up. "See you later, kid." "Goodnight, Cowboy."

The next morning I'm up before daylight. I don't know why. I guess that's what cowboys do. I go outside onto the front steps, and I wonder if there will be a pony at the party. *Thank you, Lord, that I'm so blessed.* I feel another great adventure coming today. I see lights on next door at my friend's house. I walk to the edge of the yard. It's my friend and his father. "Good morning," I said to them. "Where are you going so early?" "To the lake. We're going fishing. Do you want to come along?" "Yes, but I have to go to a party today. Maybe next time. Thanks, though. I hope you get a lot of fish." "See you later, cowboy," and off they go. I go back and sit on the steps. My cousin, Peach, is up and she is looking for me. She comes outside to say that I should not go fishing today. Her bedroom window is next to my friend's driveway. She could hear us talking. She also tells me that I have a boy cousin who is our age, and that he is in the first grade. He will be coming to the party today. Peach says that he is a baby cowboy just like me, and that he has a pony. More lights go on inside the house. I'm sure it's my uncle and he will be eating soon. Peach and I will eat with him. He wants us kids to have a good time today at the party. When our aunts wake up, they tell us that we are going shopping downtown this morning.

The party starts at noon. Everyone is excited. I play my guitar awhile before I get cleaned up and dressed.

Everyone is ready, and off to town we go. There are lots of cars and people. We go into a store to look around. Time passes quickly, and before we know it, it's party time! My aunts buy presents for the party. We drive a little way down the road, and see all the kids walking in a big yard with a big house. We get out of the car and go inside to meet everyone. What a great time! My baby cowboy cousin is here. We talk and play and I meet lots of new friends. There is lots of food. The kids are thrilled when they see a man pull up in front with a pony for the kids to ride. My aunt calls for me to come inside. She tells me one of her houses was burned half way down to the ground, and someone may be dead. We have to go back to Arkansas tomorrow. I am sad. I asked my aunt who died, but she wouldn't say. She only said that I can stay for one more week if I want, and that she will go check things out and come back for me. "Think on it, John Wayne, and let me know tonight," she said to me. "I'm packing when the party is over." "I am going back with you. You're going to need me. I can ride a pony any day." "Thank you, baby cowboy," she said to me. "I'm going with you. I miss my mama. I want to go home." "Sure, baby. You are going with me tomorrow. Now, go have fun. Cleopatra won't like it if I leave you here. She wants her baby cowboy back home."

I go back outside and the kids are having a blast. There are dancers and singers and music is all around. It is both a sad day, and a good, happy day. My uncle tells me that you have to take the good with the bad. Sure, it is sad, but life goes on. "I wish you would stay, kid," he tells me. "I'll be back next summer," I said to him. "You take care of yourself, John Wayne. I'll see you when you get back." My uncle leaves the party. He has to go on a short trip. He'll be back in a few days. I go talk to both of my cousins. I'm going to miss them. We talk about school. Everyone is in school but me. They say that school is cool, and that they learn lots of things about the world. Peach wants me to ride the pony. We go out back and wait a bit because lots of kids want to ride. There is only one pony. Some of the kids started to cry because they didn't want to ride. Peach is next, and she is excited. The man puts her on the pony and walks her around in a few circles. She loves it. She may even be a cowgirl. When she finished riding, she taught us boys how to dance. It's getting dark and the party is coming to an end. We all say goodbye, and some of the kids and I take out the trash and help clean up the place. When we get home, I pack everything for the trip back to Arkansas. I must get to sleep early, for it has been a very exciting day. I fall asleep thinking of horses and Texas Long horns.

Morning comes fast. My aunt and I take a cab to the bus station. There are not many people here this early. They load us into the bus, check our bags and off we go- back across the Texas state line. What a great time we had, and I hope I can come back next year. It's going to be a long ride back to my home. As I sit looking out of the window, I see cowboys pushing cattle down a side road. I'm thinking of the cowboy updates that I have for the sweet little old lady cowgirl. She's going to be glad to see me. I hope she needs me to shop for her. I'm falling asleep now. When I awake, we're home. It's very late. We get out, and I can see from the car lights the part of the rooming house that has burned. We go inside our home. The cab driver brings our bags inside, my aunt pays him, and off he goes. My aunt puts me to bed and tells me to sleep. She has to go next door to check things out. I'm wondering if she will tell me who died in the fire.

The next morning, I hear people and noise from next door. I'm up early most days, but I'm late today. My aunt is already outdoors, talking to workers who are rebuilding the burned parts of the house. She comes back inside to tell me to stay out of the way of the workers. She tells me I can go down the circle to the cowgirl's house. "I have talked to her earlier this morning and she's fine. She is waiting on you to come and talk story. A cowboy update is what she really needs," my aunt says to me. So I run down and around the corner, to the little old lady's house. I see joy in her face and in her eyes. We are happy to see one another. "It's been awhile, kid," she says to me. I give her a kiss. She has tears in her eyes and her glasses fog up. We talk of our cowgirl friends that have gone to heaven. She tells me that her son will be coming soon, to take her to his home upstate. She holds my hand and tells me the kid died in the fire. The mother and daughter are all right. *How sad*, I'm thinking to myself. The cowgirl also says that the fire was accidental. "No one is to blame, baby cowboy," she says. "I need you to go shop for me." She writes a long list of items she needs. She goes back inside to get money, when a few of the kids in the circle walk by on their way to the store. We say hello. I tell them that maybe I'll join them later. In the meantime, the cowgirl is back with the money, and off to the store I go.

I must go and see Cleopatra and the kids later today. I'm in the store, and I see kids getting things for school. I look out of the window and see Reverend Jones and one of his great Danes in the parking lot. He's going to let some kids ride. I'd like to, but I can't today. I have too much to do. I finish shopping and off I go. The cowgirl and I eat lunch and talk for hours. She is getting tired, so she thanks me and we say good day. I go home, and my aunt talks to me about the accident and the kid who died. After a little while, I go to my mama's house. I ride my bike to get there faster. When I get to the house, no one is home. I ride around and play with some of the kids. The gates to the school playgrounds are locked. So, we play football in the street across from the school house. Soon I see my mother, sisters, and brother coming from down the road. They see me playing football and are happy that I made it back home. They have been downtown shopping for school. I take the bags from my mother and baby sister. I say goodbye to my friends, and get my bike and ride alongside Cleopatra. When we get inside, my mother gives me a kiss, and shows me things she has for my first day in school. My baby sister will be going to school next year. She's getting excited just watching my big sister and me.

While mother is getting ready to cook, she hands me the baby. I see that he is getting big. He will be walking soon. My mother and the girls want a cowboy update. We eat and talk for hours. I play with my sister for awhile and then I head back home to my aunt's house. I'm riding and thinking of the joy in my mother's and my sister's eyes when we first saw each other today. Oh, how I missed them. I've never been apart from them for so long. They really missed me, too. It is good to be back home, although, I really miss the Lone Star State. I have a feeling I am going to be going back to Texas soon.

When I get home, I have my aunt call Rex. He picks up, and right away he knows that John Wayne must be back in town. She gives me the phone and we catch up on things; we cowboy update. He gives me Billy Bob's number and I call him. No one answers, but I'm sure we will get together real soon. I missed those boys, and I often thought of them when I was away. I'm sitting in my room about to play my guitar, when I think of the horses, down past the train tracks. I'll have to check them out tomorrow. I play awhile, then fall asleep dreaming of Texas wild mustangs, and big, Long horn cattle and all the great people that I got a chance to meet. *Oh, what a blessing. Thank you, Lord.*

Morning comes fast. My aunt is still sleeping as I fill my canteen. I get my bike, and go scouting for horses. I think of the horses out by the fruit stand, and wonder if anyone has been riding them. As I ride for awhile, I come to the country store. This time, I get apples instead of carrots. I have the shopkeeper cut the apples for me, since my aunt won't let me carry a knife. I'm riding and wishing I could see the horses. I'll try the bottom pasture first. I stash my bike in the bush. I walk down the hill through the trees. I see lots of tracks, but there's not a pony in sight. So, I climb a tall tree for a better view. *There they are! What a wonderful sight to see!* They are running, and kicking and playing. I don't see any people around. I want to go closer, but I am trespassing on someone's land. I'm thinking, long and hard, of what will happen if I get caught fooling around with horses that don't belong to me. *Go for it,* I tell myself. I walk deeper into the woods where the tall trees are. Now I will have a better view. I climb up the tree easily. It has lots of big branches. I go as high as I can without falling, and I see the horses. I sit in the tree top, eating apples and drinking water. I wait awhile, and still don't see any people. I climb back down the tree, and ease my way very close to the horses. They see me. I stop, and then start to eat more of the apple. They hear me, and see me eating. Slowly, they walk to me. I think to myself, *The first one that goes for the apple is the one I will ride*. The bay-looking pony eats from my hand, and I string-rope his neck and lead him away, down to the creek. He has mud all over his body. I wore two tee-shirts this morning, so I remove one, and wet it in the water. Then, I begin to wash the horse. It takes awhile, but all the mud comes off. I lead him down through the woods and jump on his back. We walk back, nice and easy, to my bike. I ease myself down from his back and give him more of the apple. I pet the pony on his head. What a great pony he is! I take my string rope from around his neck and begin to leave. The pony starts to follow me. He follows me until I reach my bike at the edge of the fence line. I go under the fence. The pony likes apples. So, I get the other apple from the bag on my bike and cut it on the side of a rock, then I give the pony another bite. He is standing and waiting, and I'm thinking how nice it would be if I could put a saddle on his back. I say goodbye to the pony, and off I go, up the tracks to my right, across into another pasture where I had seen lots of horses before. I put my bike behind a bush, so no one can see it. I have only one apple left. I wish I had more. I don't see any fresh horse tracks, so I look for a tree- taller than the one before. I find such a tree a little ways down the trail. I start my climb, and I'm to the top in no time. I see lots and lots of horses- many more than I saw here before! I stay in the tree, so no one can see me. I sit awhile, then notice a bird's nest next to me. I can look to my left and see baby birds in their nest. This is the first I've seen of baby birds. I don't see the mother. Maybe she is out food-shopping for her babies. I don't think it's a good thing if the mother sees me so close to the nest. So, I climb down slowly. I see the pony that I'd like to catch and ride. He is close to the tree line, but a short walk ahead. I walk easy, so I don't spook the herd of horses. But, they saw, heard, and smelled me coming toward them. They start to move, and then begin to run fast. They are kicking, and bucking and jumping all around. What a wonderful sight to see! It doesn't look like I'm going to catch any of these horses today. They have gone too far out of my reach. It's getting late, so I start my walk back to my bike, and then back home I go.

It's hot, so I stop at the country store. I buy some ice cream, and think that I'll bring more apples next time I come to see the horses. I'm almost home, when I see many horses to my right, down across the train tracks. I've never seen these horses before. I wonder to myself how many horses there could be on all this land. I will bring some apples and have a meet-and-greet with these horses soon. I make it home and my aunt kisses me. She missed me and wants a baby cowboy update, and we talk for hours. I eat, and then take a bath. My aunt tells me that the men working on the house should be finished in a few weeks. She also tells me that she has gotten a call from the Black cowboy race trackers. They will be coming to town next month. That is great news for me! I am going to see race horses again real soon. My aunt tells me that I can only go to the racetrack on weekends, since I'll be in school five days a week. I say goodnight to my aunt, and off I go, to my room. I play my guitar for awhile until I fall asleep.

Early the next day, Rex and Billy Bob want to get together and ride. Rex and his mother will pick me up at ten this morning. I get dressed and ready. I am thrilled, thinking of the adventure that lies ahead. I look out of the window and I see the big kid from next door. This is the first time I have seen him since I've come back from Texas. He's a big boy now, and has lots of things to do, places to go, and people to see. Rex is pulling up in front. I jump in the car and off we go. We are so glad to see one another! They want to know what Texas is like. We talk all the way to Billy Bob's house. Billy Bob is outside waiting for us. His parents are working, and he is happy to see us. He tells me that his body feels fine, and he feels one hundred percent better. As we arrive to Rex's ranch, we share lots of cowboy updates. The boys are happy that I'll be going to school this year. They want to know if I met any cowboys. I told them I did.

When we get to the ranch, Rex's mom makes lunch for us baby cowboys. We eat, then run to the barn. We saddle three horses and ride off, down through the pasture. Rex tells us that his dad sold the mother and baby pony to a farm up the road. We can go see them, but it's too far to ride today on horseback. We ride to the lake instead. When we get near, we see two older cowgirls coming toward us in the next pasture. We ask Rex if he knows the girls. He says no. We say hello and talk over the fence awhile. The girls are in high school. They tell us that they are going to be in the state fair and that we should come to the show. We said we would if we could. They rode off. These were the first real cowgirls I ever saw on a pony. My sweet little old lady cowgirls were my first, but by the time we met, their riding days were all over. That's why, when they met me, they said they would live out their last cowgirl days through the eyes of a baby cowboy. "And it's you, Cellulose John Wayne Jay!" the ladies said to me.

Billy Bob, Rex and I tied our horses to a tree. We're going for a swim. We swim in our underwear. I'm not a great swimmer, so I stay close to the bank. My pals swim halfway across the lake, and then turn around and swim back to me. *Man, those boys are good!* We sit on the bank and talk of many things for hours. It's getting late, so we head back to the ranch, talking of Texas mustangs and Texas Longhorn cattle. What a wonderful day it is to ride with my pals.

As soon as we arrive back to the ranch, we unsaddle the horses and give them a good bath, with lots of soap and water. The horses are happy. They know that we love them. We brush them all over, in the sunlight, so they dry faster. We clean the stalls in the barn. Then, we bed them down for the night with clean fresh water to drink, and some good hay. Then we make sure the stall door is locked. We go inside and cowboy update with the parents. They are glad that we all had a chance to hang out before school starts. This time, Rex's father takes us home. We pass my house to drop Billy Bob off first, so we could have more time to talk. My aunt is outside when we get back. Rex and his father get out of the car. Rex and I go inside, while his father stays and talks to my aunt. I play a song on my guitar for Rex. He is impressed, and tells me that he plays the drums. Maybe one day we could have a band. We say goodbye, and off he and his father go. My aunt and I stay up talking of my day's adventure. She is happy to have me home with her, but she says Cleopatra wants me to move back home. The school is right across the street. Plus, I have to start babysitting my little brother. She says I have to do more than just be a baby cowboy.

I'm getting excited about the thought of going to school. I say good night, and off to sleep I go. The night flies by, and morning comes fast. I dreamed of the little old lady cowgirls last night, and of past conversations, and the happy eyes the ladies had when we met. I get dressed and go around the circle. I see a strange looking car in front of the cowgirl's house. I knock on the door and a man comes out. "Hello! You must be Cellulose John Wayne Jay. My mother has told me all about you. I'm going to take her home today- back to Mississippi. We think it is the best thing we can do for her. She is old and frail, and this house is too big for her. No one is here to give her the care she needs. So, you see, baby cowboy, we've just got to go. Mother is taking a bath now, and I'm packing for her. I'm just taking a few things for now. I'll be back next month to get the rest. Mother is very sad, for she knows how much she is going to miss this place. Cowboy, this is my wife. She wants to talk to you." "Hello, young lady," I say to her. "Howdy, cowboy," she answered. "I've heard so much about you. We thank you for all you have done for my mother-in-law. She thinks the world of you, and wishes that she could kidnap you." Just then, my cowgirl friend comes into the room- happy to see me, for what could be the last time we see one another. She has tears in her eyes and her glasses fog up as she hugs and kisses me. Tears are rolling slowly down her face as she tells me, "I love you, baby cowboy. Through you, we cowgirls could live out the rest of our cowgirl days, here with you, in the circle of peace and love. For that, I thank you, for all the cowgirls." I help the son take the bags to the car, and his wife helps my friend into the back seat. And just like that, they drive off into the Arkansas morning- maybe never to return.

I think of my little friend who died in the fire. We were going to walk to school together and grow up together. Now, he is in heaven. The first pony I ever rode, Big White, is also in heaven. The little old lady cowgirls might all be gone soon. Billy Bob is a blessed baby cowboy because he came close to death when Big White fell through the fence and broke his leg.

I go back home, and my aunt tells me to stay around the house today. She needs my help for a few hours. The phone rings, and it's Rex. "Billy Bob and his parents are over, and they tell us that they are going to build a swimming pool at their home from the sale of their horses. And since you can't swim at the city pool, you can swim at their house day or night." "Thank you, boys." And I go help my aunt work around the house. I play my guitar awhile until it's time to eat. Time is passing fast.

CHAPTER SEVEN

The next day, I move some of my things to my mother's house. I'll have to stay over on school nights. Cleopatra needs me, more than ever, now that she has two kids that will be going to school Monday (that's tomorrow), and two kids that will have to go to the babysitter. No daddy is around, and my mother makes thirteen dollars a week. She's got to feed us, pay rent, water, light and gas bills out of her pay. And we never go without food. What a cowgirl. We never feel poor. We have lots and lots of love. My mother is so glad to see me. She kisses me. I tell her that I have another trip to make to my aunt's house This time I'll bring my bike and one of my guitars. My sisters are next door, playing with the kids. My baby brother is sleeping. My mother will take me to school tomorrow. My aunt is happy for me. When I return, she hugs and kisses me. She knows that I'll be by to see her every evening.

As I go home to Cleopatra- my original cowgirl- she's so happy that her baby cowboy is coming back home to stay. She feeds me, and we talk for hours. My sisters come in from next door. I kiss them and tell them how much I love them. The girls tell me that one leg, one arm, lots of hair and one finger have fallen off of their dolls. As the day comes to an end, my mother and my big sister try to tell me what to expect on my first day of school. We are so glad that tomorrow is the big day. I recall what happened last year, when I thought I would be in school- but they told my mother I had to wait because my birthday is in November. What a jaw dropper that was. I'm seven-years-old now and I should be in the second grade, but I'll only be in the first. We all go to sleep early. I lay in bed but I can't sleep. I'm excited about many things. I know that I need to rest, for I have a big day ahead of me tomorrow. I think of horses, and I drift slowly off to sleep.

Early to rise, I hear my baby brother yelling. He must be ready to eat. I go to check on him, and my mother has him now. She tells me to get dressed. I'll have to walk down the street with her and the babies to the sitter's house. We get ready, and off we go. It's only about five blocks

48

down the road. We drop the kids off, and head back home. My big sister is getting ready for school. We eat, and off across the street we go. My sister says goodbye and goes to class. My mother and I go into the office. They know me from last year. They talk to my mother for a short time. Then, the principal walks us to first grade and we meet the teacher. We are early, so there are not many kids here yet. My mother kisses me, and she and the principal leave me in the hands of my new babysitter. I look at her and she looks at me. "Take a seat, son," she says to me. She looks as if she could be any one of the sweet little old lady cowgirls. While she's reading my paper work given to her by the principal, I look around the room. There are more kids coming to class. The teacher calls my name. I stand, as she wants all the kids to stand when their names are called. I feel like maybe I could be in love with this place they call Goldstein.

The teacher tells us that today is meet-and-greet, and that we're not going to do school work. We are just going to talk to our new classmates. Kids are still coming into the class. The teacher calls for order, and all the kids take a seat. She wants a roll call and head count. She thinks maybe there are too many students in this class. So, she tells everyone to stay in their chairs while she goes to the office to check with the principal. She leaves the room and the kids go nuts, talking and playing. Half of the kids are out of their seats and making lots of noise. I'd say we were all just being kids, and having fun with our new classmates. The teacher is back with a list of names of the kids that will have to go to another class. I'm glad that she doesn't call my name. She tells everyone to take a seat and pay attention. I like my new teacher. The teacher gives everyone a book, and tells us we are going to learn how to read. "Now for the rest of the day, I want you kids to look at every page, and tomorrow we will discuss the book. The books are yours to keep and take home." The room was as still as night; every kid was deep into their book. "Hey!" I yelled with excitement. " There are lots of horses on this page, but no words!" The teacher came over to my seat. "Do you need help, Cellulose?" she asked. "Yes ma'am, I do. Why are there no words?" "Because you students are going to write the words on every page. Is that all?" "Yes, teacher," I said.

The bell rings and the kids start to talk. The teacher tells us to put our books away. It's lunch time. "I'm going to take you kids to the lunch room. Everyone line up in a single file line by the door. Thank you," she said. *What a thrilling day*, I thought. My teacher is nice, and I like my new classmates. And, I live across the street. We walk into the lunch room, as my classmates and I follow the teacher. What a big room! There are lots of kids, sitting and eating, and it's kind of loud, with sounds of joy and happiness. I think of the things my white pals, Billy Bob and Rex, told me of their first day in school. Billy Bob goes to an all-White school. Rex goes to school with two black kids. I go to school with all-Black students. This is 1960, in the deep south. Even as a kid, I could see progress- slow- but progress. We kids get our food, then sit and eat. Kids are coming and kids are leaving. We finish and go back to class. Before I know it, the bell rings and everyone is excited. The teacher makes sure that we all have our books as we leave. I see all the new kids getting on school buses and lines of cars out front to pick up kids. Action is what I see, and I am glad to be part of it. *Thank you, Lord, that I am finally in school!* I walk across the street with the girl next door. She's in my class and we both agreed that it had been a wonderful day of school. When I get home, my sister is doing homework. She tells me we have to go to the baby sitter and pick up the babies. As we walk, we talk of school, all the action, and of all the new kids. She is going to help me with my homework later in the evening.

My mother should be home soon, and then I can go see my aunt. She must need me for something. My big sister and I get the kids. Back to the house we go. My mother is home- sooner than I thought. With happy eyes, she says hello to us kids. She can tell that we had a great day in school. The babies are happy to see their mother. As the evening flies by, I get my bike and ride to my aunt's house. She sends me across the street to the store. When I get back from shopping, we sit in the chairs out front and talk. We talk until dark and she wants me to eat, but I can't. We say goodnight, and off I go back to my mother's house. After we eat, my mother puts us all to bed very early. I didn't do my homework, but I looked the book over. It's easy.

The next day I am up early. I do my chores, get cleaned up, and get dressed for school. My mother has the day off. She will keep the babies home today. My sister and I go to school. I met a boy who has a pair of cowboy boots. I ask him if he is a cowboy. He says he is not, but that there are horses down the road from his house. He says the white owners don't like any kids playing with the horses. There are three horses in a very big pasture. He tells me that he and two boys were inside the fence playing around with the horses one day, and the owner saw them. He said the man had a gun, and started yelling at the boys to stay away from the horses, and that the next time they trespassed, he would shoot! I ask him if he could show me how to get to the horses. He tells me he can. I say to him that no other kids must know, or we could get in big trouble.

There are more new kids in my class today. The teacher tells us all to take out our book. Each kid gets a chance to name the pictures inside. After awhile, we go to lunch and then to the playground. I talk to the boy again about the horses. After school he will show me how to get to them. We must ride our bikes. I see my sister on the playground. She wants to know if things are all right. I told her that I was going scouting after school. She told me to be careful, and to be home by dark. After school, I walk very fast from class with my new friend. We go past his house. He can't go all the way to the pony pasture but he shows me the way. He has chores to do every day after school. His father has hunting dogs, and he has to handle the dogs every day and clean out their pens. He tells me that past his house to the left, down in the valley, by a big oak tree I will see the horses. I get my bike and get to the horse pasture in no time. I hide my bike. My sister and my friend told me to be careful. I don't see a pony, but I smell them. I look for tracks and I see tracks- but they're not fresh. I walk a little more and I find fresh horse manure. I know they are close. I climb a tree for a better look. I sit and wait, and shortly I see two horses not too far away. I don't see any people, so I climb down, walk to the horses, and they just stand and let me pet them. I wished I had some carrots or an apple. Next time I will bring some. I'm glad to meet new horses. I get my bike and head home. I stop at my friend's house on the way. I help him with the dogs, while telling him of my short adventure. I ask my friend if he has ever seen anyone ride the horses. "Yes. The big horses aren't wild, but I fear you may get yourself in big trouble." I head home and think to myself that one day I will ride those ponies- some day real soon.

I get home before dark and my aunt is at our house. I walk my aunt back home and stay the night. I play my guitar and think to myself about the dozen sweet little old lady cowgirls that I met in this circle of peace and love when I was four. They are no longer with us. Now, I am seven and they are in heaven. My aunt told me while walking home, that the last cowgirl died last night. She is in greener pastures in heaven, with her cowgirl friends of long ago. May they rest in peace. I fall asleep thinking of cowboy updates that we all shared together. They would always tell me to stay alert and pay attention. "You're going to get hurt in your line of work, John Wayne. It's just a matter of when. Stay on your toes around horses." I'm dreaming now. *The thoroughbreds are coming very soon. I'm excited about those race horses. It's nonstop action on the backside. I smell the barns and the fresh hay bales.* I hear birds singing outside my window and dogs barking. It's morning already. My dream was so clear. I really thought that I was on the track, in the barn, with horses all around. I jump in the bath tub, and then get dressed for school. My aunt is cooking and says we can eat soon. I hear kids walking past the house on their way to school. I eat, kiss my aunt, and off to school I go. When I get to class, there is a new student seated next to my desk. She says hello to me, and tells me that her name is Princess. She's from California.

After school, I tell my sister that I'm going to scout some ponies down by the train tracks. She tells me to be careful, and to be back before dark. I get my bike, string rope, and canteen. I'll stop and get carrots or apples at the country store. Off I go, seeking another baby cowboy adventure. As I ride, I see kids with fishing poles down by the creek. Looks like fun. Some of the kids take a swim. I pass by with ease, and no one sees me, for I am up high on the tracks. I'm almost to the country store. Maybe I can get apples and carrots. I can't feed all the horses, but I'll feed the ones I can. I put my bike on the side of the store. When I get inside, there are no fruits or vegetables today. What a let down. I promised those ponies. So, I buy a box of sugar cubes instead. I hope they like them. I get down to the first pasture on my left. I slow down, and go past to the next pasture. I roll my bike off the tracks, down to the fence. I hide my bike in the tall bush. I'm now over the fence, and walking into the woods, down by the creek. That's a good place to start scouting. There are lots of tracks, and fresh manure is everywhere. To save time, I start my climb high in a tree for a better view. I don't see a pony anywhere in sight. It's very still and nothing is moving. I stay put, and I hear the sound of wind and birds. I'm thinking maybe the horses are in another pasture down the road. I climb down the tree, get my bike, and down the road I go. I get to the next pasture and I find the same two horses as before. They walk right up to me. I give them love, and begin to rub them both. I put my string rope around one of the horse's face and head. I get a handful of hair and jump on his back. We walk slowly down through the woods. The other pony follows behind. We ride into a clearing, and the trees open up into a wonderful valley below. What a view! I look all around as far as the eye can see. Nothing is moving. It is as if these horses and I are all alone in this town. I stop, and begin to turn around. I'm thinking that maybe I'm too far out in the open. I should get back to my bike. I ease my way back down into the woods. I get off the horse and put the rope on the other pony. I ride him to the fence line where I left my bike. I pet them both on the head, and off I go.

I'm going to stop at my aunt's house. She must need me for something. I see the kids fishing. This time, they see me, and yell hello to me. They raise their arms to show me all the fish they caught. "Very good!" I yell back to them. I see two hobos coming down from the woods onto the tracks. We pass one another and no one speaks. I pick up the pace and soon I'm at my aunt's house. We're happy to see one another. We talk awhile, until she takes me over to the boarding house. The workmen have gone for the day, but they will be back tomorrow. "What do you think, baby cowboy?" she asks. "Wonderful job," I said. They won't finish until next week, just in time for the Black cowboy race trackers from all over the country. I've met some of the guys before, but my aunt tells me that some new cowboys are coming this year. My aunt and I go home. We eat and talk awhile, and then off I go to Cleopatra's house. Everyone is home. We talk, and my mother tells me that I have to go to the wash house and wash the babies' clothes. I get on my bike, and off I go to wash. It takes a couple of hours. One of my classmates and his parents are washing, also. The kid and I talk about school and kid-stuff. I finish and I hurry back home for bed.

I'm up early the next morning. My mama needs me to go to the store. The baby needs milk. I take the short cut down the hill, behind my house, through the woods and down the trail to the store. I see a few kids in the store. It's hours before school starts. I talk to the kids. They are crossing guards; they stop the cars, so the kids can walk across the streets in a safe manner. The boys tell me it's a very important job, and that when I'm in third grade, I may become a crossing guard. That's two years from now. I shop, and get the items mother sent me to get. I run up the hill, through the woods, and in the back door I go. All the kids are awake. We eat, and then my sister and I take the babies to the sitter's house. We walk to school, but this time, we take the long way around to school. We see kids leaving their homes. Some kids are from my school, and some big kids are catching the bus for high school. When we get to school, my sister and I sit on the playground until the school bell rings. Off to class we go. When I get to class, the teacher is not there yet. The kids are coming in one by one and taking their seats. My friend, Princess, is already in her chair talking to classmates. We say hello. My pal with the hunting dogs comes in, and says he will go with me the next time I go scouting for horses. "Are you sure?" I ask him. My pal likes horses, but has never ridden a pony. He knows where there are lots of horses. He goes hunting with his father, and horses are all around. He'll take me there some day after hunting season is over. Right now he says his father has a dozen hunting dogs, and six baby hunting dogs. "My brothers and I have to take good care of them everyday," he says.

The teacher arrives. She says good morning to us all and tells us to be seated. All of the kids are happy to be in school. We all want to learn lots of new things about the world. Each one of us has named all the pictures in our book. The teacher gives us each another book. We must look through the book tonight, and we will talk about the book tomorrow. When school is out for the day, I see Princess and her friends walking home. I run to catch up to them. We all walk and talk, until there is no one left but Princess and me. She says she lives across the main road. We stop at the corner. There are lots of cars and trucks coming up the road. I see race horses in the trucks. I wonder if my friends are here. I say goodbye to my classmate.

I get home and tell my sister that I'm riding my bike to my aunt's house. When I get there, she tells me the boys will be here tomorrow. She says maybe I can go to the racetrack this weekend. My aunt needs me to help her around the house and to go to the store. When I get home, my mother needs me to go shopping for her. Off I go, back to the store. This time at the store, I see Reverend Jones. He has no dogs with him today. He is shopping, and he's glad to see me. This Sunday is when he wants to see me in Sunday school class. After I finish shopping, on my way out, I tell him that my sister and I will be there Sunday for Bible study. "See you!" he yells. I get home and tell my mother that I am going to church this week. She's glad. Before I know it, it's time for bed. I'm thinking of thoroughbreds- ponies that are one of a kind. I'm thinking of action and nonstop race horses. I can't get enough! I'm in school now, but all I think about are ponies. I wonder at times if I'm sick! I fall asleep thinking of the first race horse that I will ride.

The next morning, I do my chores and get ready for school. When I get to class, the teacher has new books. We are learning how to read, write and count. All the kids are excited about the new books. We all study our books until lunch time. After lunch, the teacher wants to check our homework from yesterday. She tells the class that most days we will have homework. The bell rings and school is out. I have chores to do. Then, I have to go to my aunt's house. I'll take my books with me, so I can do my homework there.

When I get to my aunt's house, the race trackers are there. We are all glad to see one another. My aunt cooks for the cowboys and me. We sit around the table eating, and getting caught up with our cowboy updates. Three new cowboys are here this year. The boys say they have more horses this time than before. They are happy that I go to school now. They say I can go to the track any day that I'm not in school. *Sounds good to me!* The wranglers and my aunt need me to go to the store across the street. I see the big kid from next door. He has a new bike, and wants to give me his old one. His old bike is much nicer than mine. I tell him thanks, and I will be over when I finish shopping. I don't need two bikes. I think that I will give my bike to the new kid who just moved into the circle last week. I get back from shopping and I finish eating dinner. I go next door to my friend's house. He gives me the bike, and he and I ride around until almost dark. I like my new wheels and I thank my friend. We both have homework, so we say goodnight. I go inside and say goodnight to my aunt and the race trackers. They tell me to have a good day in school tomorrow. I do my homework and play my guitar. I fall asleep, and when I wake up, it's one o'clock in the morning. I'm dreaming of race horses talking to one another, kicking the stall doors. They want out! They are ready to work and to train on the track. I fall back to sleep. I hear the cowboys leaving for work, but I stay in bed. I need more sleep. I have to be fresh and alert this morning for school. Cleopatra has told me many times that there is more to life than horses. I am thinking maybe so, but, I never dream of anything else but a pony.

I'm up and finished with my chores. I get cleaned up, dressed, eat a little, and have a glass of milk. I see the big kid from next door. We walk to school together and more kids join us. We get to school early. All the kids are playing, talking, doing homework, and two boys are fighting. The bell rings and they stop fighting. Once seated, we find out that we get out of school early today because teachers have a meeting. *This is great news!* I will go pony scouting and I'll ask my classmate with the hunting dogs to come along. We could walk the dogs and ride a pony. My classmate, Princess, overhears my friend and me talking. She tells us we should stay out of trouble. "We will," I replied. The bell rings, school is out, and my friend says to meet him at the gas station in one hour. I tell him I will go to the school lunch room and get some apples and carrots for the horses. Then I'll go home and get my string rope halter- the special string rope that the little old lady cowgirls gave me when I made my first stick pony- back on the day when they started missing their brooms and mops from their back steps. They asked me if I knew anything about their missing brooms and mops. I answered "Yes," and the rest is history. I get my canteen, my rope, the apples and carrots. Off I go, down the hill, behind my house, through the woods and down to the gas station. I stop and put air in my bike tires. Then I rush down behind the station to the creek. My friend is already waiting with the hunting dog. With happy eyes, we take off on what I hope to be another legendary day in the life of a baby cowboy. We have a few miles to go. I'm riding and thinking that we will sit in the tree top and make sure that the owner is not there. If he's there, we can out-wait the man. We get to the pasture, and stash our bikes in the tall grass, so as not to be seen by anyone. My friend's dog is very well trained, and makes no noise. As soon as we get to the trees, we see lots of big thoroughbreds. Once you see those beautiful creatures, you never forget what they look like. We're just kids looking for a pony to ride- not a race horse. I want to find the two horses I saw my last trip out here. They will be safe horses for us to ride. "You've never been on a pony," I say to my friend. "and a race horse is not what we need." So as not to spook the herd, we tie the dog to the tree and climb to the top. Suddenly, the horses appear, walking along the creek bed very close to us. We look down the road to the main gates of the pasture. We don't see anyone. We climb down, and I tell my pal to stay with the dog. I walk down through the woods to where the horses are taking a drink from the creek. I have a carrot in my hand. They see the carrot and walk right to me. I give them two carrots each. I string rope the pony and walk to my pal. The other pony follows. He wants more carrots. I help my friend up on the horse's back- just as the white hobo man helped me onto my first pony. I walk around in big circles for half an hour with the kid. He is having a very good time on his first pony ride! I help my pal down from the horse. We sit under the tree and feed the rest of the apples and carrots to the horses. I've never been on this other pony. Now is a good time to try him. I look around for vines, and find enough vines to make another string rope- a lead rope. I switch rope halters, then jump the other pony. We walk around in small circles, and he's fine. I ride him and lead my friend around on the other pony. We ride around for an hour or so. Then we hand rub the horses. We say goodbye to the horses, for now. I walk to the fence for the bikes, while my pal walks the dog down to the creek for a drink of cool water. Poor dog- he's been tied up to the tree for a long time. We just could not take a chance on him spooking the herd. We get on our bikes and off we go. We stop at the gas station again. We buy some ice cream and sit on the side of the station in the shade. My pal lives around the corner. We say goodbye, and off to my house I go. I'm thinking to myself as I ride home, that my friend must be thrilled half to death! I remember how I felt after my first pony ride. I've got to hurry home. I have chores to do, and I have to get ready for my big day tomorrow. I've got a date with some legendary Black cowboys.

When I reach home, no one is there. Then, I see Cleo and the kids walking up the street with grocery bags. I hurry to meet them. My big sister wants me to teach her how to ride a bike. I'm happy to help my sister, because all she likes is homework and dolls. She has a real baby doll brother, but plays with store bought dolls. I go outside and put the training wheels on my bike. Now my sister will not need my help. She can ride all by herself, as long as she stays on the sidewalk. I still have to help her a little. Before long, she is doing fine. I'm glad my friend gave me this bike, for it is much bigger, and easier for my sister. She has long legs. I watch her for a little while and wonder if it's time to take off the training wheels. I think I will wait a few days. Cleopatra and the kids are watching from the window. I'm thinking my baby sister, Francine, can do this. I must let her try someday soon.

Meanwhile, I have to get packed. I am going to my aunt's house for the weekend. My mother is talking to me about paying attention and staying alert, for she knows one day I'm going to get hurt- not if- but when. I take the training wheels off of my bike. I say goodbye to my family and hug and kiss my mama. Off I go to my aunt's house. When I get there, no one is around except the mailman. He has a letter for Cellulose John Wayne Jay. *Hey, that's me!* It's from Abner Wingate Jay. *Hey, that's my daddy!* The mailman gives me the letter. I sit on the steps out front and open the letter. It's a picture of my daddy and his new banjo. He made it all by himself. His handwriting is not clear, but I do understand him asking of Cleo and the girls. My aunt is coming home from the store across the street. She helps me read the letter. Abner says he loves us and misses us. He can't wait to see us- hopefully very soon. He tells me to try and stay light on my toes around the horses. I sit and wonder. My mother and sisters will be so happy to get this letter. I tell my aunt that I'll be back. I have to get this letter to Cleopatra. I rush back home with happy eyes. I jump off my bike while it's still rolling. I push the front door open and give the letter to my mother. She is very happy to see me. She thinks I'm coming back home to stay. "Here's a letter from my daddy!" I give her the letter. There's another paper inside the letter. My mother tells me it's a check for three-hundred dollars. I'm in the first grade and I can count. Now, I know Cleo makes thirteen dollars a week in pay, so three-hundred dollars is a lot of paydays. My mama yells, "Thank you, Lord!" She kisses me, and off I go back to my aunt's house.

When I arrive at her house, I look out my window and see the cowboys. I run two doors down to the rooming house. "Hey, it's the stick horse baby cowboy! Hey kid, how are you?" "It's been awhile," I say to the cowboys. "I'm going with you in the morning." "Yes, we kind of figured that you would. You've gotten taller. Get some sleep, John Wayne. We go before the chickens are up." "See you, cowboys." Off I go, back home. I was thrilled! I had looked those old boys deep in their eyes, and begun to think of my cowgirls in heaven and the look they had in their eyes- of slowing down, heading out to greener pastures. Three of the race trackers are younger men who have never been here before. I'm thinking that most of these old boys are, most likely, on their last rendezvous. This could be the last time I see these legendary Black cowboys. I sure hope not, but you have to stay light on your toes around these race horses. Now I looked those old boys over real good and they are moving much slower than before. Yes, I see these cowboys riding slowly off into the sunset. I fall off to sleep. I dream of a pony.

Morning comes fast. I'm outside sitting on the front steps and I see the cowboys coming for me. "Howdy, John Wayne!" "Morning, fellows. Good to see you!" We get in the car and off we go to the racetrack. It's very early in the training season. There aren't many horses on the track yet. In a few months all the barns will be filled with race horses. Some of God's most fabulous creatures on earth are here. As we drive through the gate, the guard waves for us to enter. I'm so excited! I hear, smell, feel and see thoroughbreds. I rush to get the feed cart. We load bags of feed and hay. The cowboys are taking the long water hoses down and around the barn. After I feed, I clean all the water buckets and refill them with clean water. The cowboys are cleaning the stalls. First they remove all the straw and mop up all the wet spots. Then, fresh new straw is put down. It's nice and fluffy and at least three feet high. After the horses eat, the hot walkers come in. They start walking the horses around the inside of the barn. This year, they have more hot walkers- both man and machine. We have forty horses in this barn and forty horses in the barn next door. The action is nonstop. The hot walking machines are set up outside of the barns and between the barns. It's like a carousel; a merry-go-round with lead ropes to snap to the horses' heads, and pull them around in circles. They must get a good workout. Some days it gets so cold that the track freezes and it's not safe for the horses to train. That is why the hot walkers and the automatic hot walking machines are very, very important on a thoroughbred racetrack. It's time to saddle up. The jockeys and the exercise riders are coming into the barn. We wrap legs, we tie tongues down, we pin up tails and we put on blinker. We have some young horses in the barn this year. Some have never seen a starting gate. These cowboys have a lot of work to do. *What a thrilling adventure for a baby cowboy first grader!*

The horses are going to the track. Some days I watch them work out. Today is one of those days. There are many horses on the track this morning. I keep my eyes on the four horses from my barn. They really look good, and should be in top shape for a fast time today. The trainer is happy. It's a good workout for the horses. The boys yell for me. Our barn is right behind the track. I run down the hill to the car, and off we go. Another great morning of hanging out with a herd of wonderful thoroughbred race horses and all the Black legendary wild horse wranglers. I got a chance to see the boys in action. Some of these men I may never see again, after this year's meet. I'm feeling sad just thinking about it. We're back home now and the cowboys go back to feed at three o'clock today. They say that I can go, if I want. I think I'm just going to be a kid for the rest of the day. "Hey kid, you done good today, John Wayne," the boss wrangler says to me. "Peace."

I run home. My aunt is excited and meets me at the front door. She hugs and kisses my face. We talked for hours. I go to take a bath, eat and take a rest. I sit on my bed, and the phone rings. My aunt calls to me. It's my little white baby cowboys calling. They want to come and pick me up today. That's fine, but I have to sleep right now. I'll be ready at three o'clock. "We'll see you then, John Wayne." I fall asleep a happy and blessed kid. *Thank you, Lord.*

Today I am going to take my new Texas saddle with me to my friend's ranch. They have lots of saddles, but I want my pals to see my first Texas saddle that I used to ride my first Texas mustang pony. A loud car horn blows. It's the baby cowboys and their parents. They all come inside and talk a bit, and then we eat ice cream. They like my saddle and they want to use it. They put it in the car. Rex's mother loves her handmade saddle, and says that she loves mine as well. Off we go to the ranch. It's not far, and we are there in no time. We run to the barn. We get three horses out. When we finish putting on the saddles, we clean out the stalls and give them clean, fresh water to drink. Rex has a new dog. We will take the dog out on the trail with us. We check our gear and off into the sunset we baby cowboys ride. Slow and easy, we ride up and down the wonderful, rolling grass hills. We stop after awhile and tie the horses to a tree. We sit and talk, and eat apples. We give the horses one apple to split between them. They are happy for the treat. The boys are happy in school, and so am I. I tell them of all my new classmates and of the horses I met on and off the racetrack. We just don't have enough time to discuss more cowboy updates. The sun is setting. We must turn back. We have a few miles to go. Billy Bob wants us to come to his house tomorrow. We can go for a swim. His pool has a heater, and he says we can swim all night if we like. His parents will come and pick me up at the same time, at the same place.

We make it back to the ranch just before dark. We unsaddle and brush the horses down well. Then we bed them down properly. "Goodnight, boys," we say to the horses. We go inside and get cleaned up for dinner. The parents are so happy that we could get together today. With school in session, the boys are very busy and don't have much spare time to play. Billy Bob is taking piano classes. He is very excited about music. Billy Bob's mother has three tickets for us boys. Elvis is back, and we are going to see his movie at the mixed picture show next week. It's getting late, and I must go to the track in the morning. I've got a date with some race horses. Off we go to my house. I thank my pals and Billy Bob's parents for a wonderful day. They say to me, "Thank you, baby cowboy. You know we love you." "Peace."

I run into the house with happy eyes. I'm ready to give my aunt all the baby cowboy updates that she can handle. She wants me to eat but I've already eaten, so we sit and talk for what seemed like hours. I wake up in my bed the next morning, but I don't know how I got there. I get dressed and out the door I go. The lights are on at the rooming house. The cowboys will be out soon. It starts to rain a little. I rush back inside to get my rain gear. When I come out of the house, the boys are calling for me. As we drive, it rains harder. I love the rain. The boss tells us it's going to be a short morning workout. There is no guard at the gate this morning, but we do have guards in the barns. The rain has stopped. Suddenly somebody yells, "Pony down!" Men run to the back stall. A pony is sick. He's down and he can't get up. The cowboys work on him a few seconds, then they pull the pony up by rope and walk him around, and after about an hour the pony is fine. We finish feeding and doing chores. It's time to saddle a few horses, and we walk the horses that are not going to the track today. There are lots of new race horses coming in this morning. I run outside to see; I love to watch the horses load and unload. The jockeys are here and one of the pony boys is going to let me ride his pony horse around the barn. His pony is an ex-race horse. His job is to lead the race horses around he track. I jump the pony horse, and we walk easy around the barn. What a thrill! This was my first thoroughbred ride of my young life, and I made sure that I stayed alert and paid attention. From stick horses to real horses- this was the real thing. What a wonderful day in the life of a baby cowboy! The men that brought me to the track are ready to head back. Their job is over for today. The other boys stay until noon. I thank the boys for setting it up so I could ride my first race horse. "Any time, John Wayne. You know we love you, cowboy!"

I take a good rest when I get home. Later, I'll go for a swim at Billy Bob's house. The boys don't know it, but Billy Bob and I are going to play some music today. I am taking my guitar. I think I'll tune up and play awhile until the baby cowboys get here. My aunt needs me to go to the store. When I get back, Rex and Billy Bob are waiting for me out front. I hurry inside with the items from the store. I get my guitar, kiss my aunt, and off we go. What a great day for a swim. It's not a hot day, but the pool is heated. Billy Bob's house is only ten miles away, so we get there fast. We jump from the car and run through the yard. The barn is no longer here. The pool is where the barn used to be. After Billy Bob and his horse, Big White, fell through the fence, his mother sold the rest of the horses. Now they have a big, beautiful pool. And, they are going to let me swim today, and any day that I wish. I often think of Big White, for he was the first pony I ever rode. I also think of how the sweet little old lady cowgirls told me what to do, and how I should ride that pony. They had no idea that a Hobo would be helping me with my first pony ride.

The boys and I change into our swim trunks. The parents come out to bring food and drinks. They take pictures as we jump into this very large pool. I find it to be almost the size of the Black pool back in town where I swim. The parents say to me, "John Wayne, maybe you can't swim at the all-White pool in town, but you are always welcome to swim here." "Yes, I will," I tell them. "Thank you very much." The water is ten feet deep. I swim close to the edge of the pool. I'm not a great swimmer, but I will be soon, now that I have lots of room to move my arms and legs, and I can see the bottom. What a thrill! Rex and Billy Bob are on the diving board. They yell for me to come give it a try. This should be easy compared to jumping from my grandmother's second-story window. The boys are jumping up and down on the board. Suddenly, there's a big splash! They jumped together. My pals are having a great time. I go next. This is my first dive ever from a board! I jump on the board a few times and then, "Splash!" I hit the water fast with my eyes closed, and water is in my nose. I'm all shook up, like Elvis. I come up kicking, and sucking for air with my eyes wide open. I hear Billy Bob's daddy saying, "Keep kicking, cowboy, and swing your arms and pull the water back to your body with your hands, real fast, like we did at the lake. Remember, you're in ten feet of water. You're doing good, kid!" "I'm swimming!" I yelled. I make it to the side and take a rest. I like this, and I'll have to get in shape. I don't like water in my nose. We get out and dry off. The food is ready and we eat and talk. All of a sudden, we hear a loud horn from a car or truck. We turn around, and it's a big horse van. What a surprise! Today is Rex's ninth-birthday. His mother has the man from next door bring three horses from the barn so that we can take a ride down by the fence where Billy Bob and Big White got hurt. The men get the horses unloaded, and they already have the saddles on, and the heads set. We jump the ponies and off we go, slow and easy. Billy Bob's mother has planted a tree and some flowers in the spot where Big White fell. We ride over the still, green grass and although it's almost winter, the rolling hills are beautiful. The leaves are falling and the colors are fabulous. We cowboys are riding into the sunset. The boys are happy, and so am I. We turn around and head for home. What a blessed day. *Thank you Lord, for another wonderful adventure in the life of a baby cowboy.* We're almost back to the pool, and the boys want to swim again. The parents take care of the horses while we play in the pool. We talk about school, splash around, and then get out of the warm water. Now we feel the chill bumps as we run to the house. We dry off and change back into our cowboy gear. We sit and eat, then say goodnight to Billy Bob and his parents. We thanked them for a great time. "Peace." As we leave, the horse van is leaving. They drop me off at home, and I wish my pal Rex another happy birthday. "Thanks for everything, cowboy," I tell him. "See you soon." And off they go, back to the ranch.

My aunt meets me at the door. We sit and talk for hours until she tells me to get some rest because I've got another big day tomorrow- it's called Monday. She kisses me and I fall asleep dreaming of wild horses in Texas. I think they must be mustangs. "Click-clack, click-clack," it sounds as though they are right outside my window. I jump up and look outside, when I realize I was having a nightmare. I was just dreaming. There are no horses outside. I fall back to sleep. I hear the cowboys. Everyone is up. I rush outside to say hello to the cowboys. They know that I have to go to school. They tell me to pay attention and to have a great day. "See you, cowboys." I rush back inside to sleep, and daylight comes fast.

Before long, I'm back in class and the teacher is telling us to pay attention. I find myself halfway paying attention, and thinking of wild horses running fast and free alongside the Texas Long horn cattle. The teacher calls for me to come and pass out some new books. I give my classmate, Princess, the first book. She is so smart and can read very well. Once everyone has a book, the teacher tells us to open to page one, and the lesson begins. The morning goes by fast. It's lunch time, and I look for my pal. He may want to go pony scouting today. We can't talk much in class and my pal sits in the back of the class. I see him, and go to his lunch table. He says he can't go scouting today because he has music class after school. Princess sits down with us. She wants to show us a letter that she's writing to the teacher. We are impressed. She writes like a sixth grader. She says that she will help us any time we need help, and that she is going to be a teacher when she grows up. The bell rings and we go the playground. Some kids are talking, some are reading and some are playing baseball and football. I'm just standing and watching, waiting for school to end. I just want to ride a pony. That's all I can think about right now. The bell rings and playtime is over. The kids slowly walk back to class. The teacher calls for me again to pass out more new books. We have a total of three books each. Our homework for tonight is to look over the new books. Also, everyone has to be able to count to fifty. It's a fast moving day and the sun is setting early this time of year. That means I can't stay out after dark scouting for ponies. I don't have enough daylight. The bell rings. School is out for the day. Cleopatra tells me all the time that there is more to life than riding a pony. So, I think maybe I won't go looking for a pony today.

Instead, I ride my bike up the sidewalk to the White boarding house where the fruit and vegetable stand is. I think of my thirteen boss ladies and one ex-boss man of not so long ago. They are in heaven and I'm seven. The son is taking over the boarding house and fruit stand. He wants me to work this summer, like I did for his mom and dad. I say "Yes," with happy eyes, because that's the only way I can see those horses deep in the woods, down behind the country fruit stand. It's been awhile since I was there. It's much too far to walk or ride my bike. I only hope the horses are still there. If so, they don't know of all the apples and carrots they are going to get to eat this summer! There are new people here now, and lots of kids. I think about the sweet little old lady cowgirls as I ride the circle on my bike, passing their old houses. I think of that day when they said to me, "Cellulose John Wayne, you are a fabulous shepherd for the Lord's flock of ponies around the nation. What a sensation! We love you, baby cowboy!" I have to stop day dreaming and get home.

Cleopatra is waiting for me. I have homework to do tonight if I want to learn to read as well as my little classmate, Princess. I ride my bike fast and silently say *thank you* to the big kid next door who gave me his bike. It's like a new bike.

The next day in school, my pal tells me we can walk two dogs after school today. That's baby cowboy code talk, because we could not let the other kids know that we are law breakers and trespassers. We could also be called baby cowboy horse thieves. I must pay attention in class today. It's becoming a problem to pay attention in class when all I think of are horses. The teacher wants everyone to take a test today. The lunch bell rings. I walk to lunch with some of the kids, but I can't eat. So, I sit and talk. Lots of kids are going to the movies this weekend. So am I. I've got a date with two baby cowboys and Elvis. Although we will be in the same movie house, the Whites will sit on the first floor and the Black kids will sit up top. But, we will be able to see the same movie, at the same time, in the same movie house. My classmate will be hunting, and I think I will ask my friend, Princess, to go with me and the cowboys. The bell rings and we go to the playground. When we get back to class, the teacher tells us that starting next Monday, the first graders will take a nap for one-half-hour each day. I think this is great news! I'm going to need a rest, so I can stay alert, and pay more attention to the horses my pal and I are going to ride. The teacher asks each student to go to the chalk board and write our name, and write from one to fifty.   After we finish, the teacher gives us homework. The bell rings and school is out. Out the door we go.

I rush home and get my gear. I didn't eat lunch today, but I did get carrots and apples from my classmate's lunch trays for the horses. I get my bike and off I go. I keep in mind as I ride that darkness comes early. I see my pal crossing the highway with two wonderful hunting dogs. We meet behind the gas station. I hold the dogs and my pal goes into the station. He comes out with two candy bars. We eat as we ride our bikes, leading a hunting dog each, down behind the gas station and through the woods. If the creek looks safe enough to cross, we will take the short cut up the road, and over the ridge. We see the fence line. The dogs are sweet. They don't make any noise. We hide the bikes, and under the wire we go. We go to the stream. We don't see any horses, but we do see many fresh tracks. We keep walking, until the dogs smell pony. They don't bark, so they won't run the herd off. "Very smart dogs you have, kid," I say to my pal. "Thanks," he answers. We see the horses and there are more than before. I must think fast. I take one carrot and tell my pal to stay with the dogs. I walk slow and easy to the herd. All heads turn as I get closer and closer. A few of the horses walk away and some run away. So, I show the carrots. I snap the carrot in half. I really have their attention now. They stand still as I reach my hand out slowly. The black and white spot pony grabs the bait carrot, and the string rope is around his neck. He's caught, so I give him the rest of the carrot. I'm leading him back to my pal. Five horses are following us. I have enough apples and carrots in the bag on my bike. My pal is so excited to see me come walking through the woods with one string rope, and six of God's most marvelous creatures! He has tied the dogs to a tree and he's got the apples and carrots ready. For safety reasons, we back out through the wire fence and then feed the horses, so as not to get stepped on. The horses rush the fence to eat. They love it! I only wish I had more apples and carrots. I jump the pony. He is not wild. We walk around in small circles. He handles very well. I slide off and help my pal aboard. He is thrilled! The pony has a very wide back. I cut the circle a little too fast and almost lost the kid. I tell him to hold on. After a short while, we rub the pony down. We only wish we had more time, and over the wire we go. We ride fast on our bikes. The dogs are happy and strong. They pull us up the hill, down around the bend and through the woods. I see the gas station. I think we might stop for ice cream. I go inside while my pal holds the dogs. I want to get two ice cream bars but I only have enough money for one. So, we split the ice cream bar. I cross the highway with my pal and the dogs. We say goodbye. I rush home before dark, thinking of all the homework I have to do for tomorrow.

Cleopatra gets home and wants me to go to the wash house down the sidewalk from the fruit stand. This is good, because I think that maybe I can talk to the Black cowboys if they are home. My aunt will be glad to see me. She knows I can't stay away for long. I get my bike and off I go. While the wash is washing, I go down to my aunt's house. "Hello, cowboy. Would you like to eat?" she asks. "Yes, ma'am," I answer. I tell her that school is going well, and that Cleo and the kids are good. My aunt needs me to help her around the house one day this weekend. I better go check the wash. I go inside the wash house and one of my classmates is there with his mother. I put my wash in the dryer and talk a bit before going back to my aunt's house. She wants me to take the leftover food down to the rooming house for the cowboy race trackers to eat. When I get there, the boys are playing cards, smoking, drinking, and talking about girls. We are thrilled to see one another! They want a cowboy update. They tell me how much they have missed me on the racetrack. I tell them I have missed them as well. I have to go check the wash, and the dryer has stopped. I fold, stack, and bag the clothes and off I go. I go to my aunt's and drop off the wash. I go back to talk to the cowboys. After about an hour, we say goodnight and I go back and hug and kiss my aunt. Then, I go home for the night.

I'm up early the next morning. I get dressed and go out back and sit on the steps. It's still dark. I'm thinking of the horses down by the train tracks. I need to see them. I'm starting to notice how still it is. Nothing is moving. I rush back inside. It's one o'clock in the morning. I'm up much too early for school. I undress and go back to bed. When I get to school, the teacher tells us that school is out for first graders at noon today. That is great news for me! Maybe I can go with the cowboy race trackers at three o'clock and see the feeding process. Or, maybe I'll go down the train tracks to see some horses I haven't seen in awhile.

My pal is still thrilled about our little adventure with the hunting dogs and the horses. He wants to go see Elvis this weekend. My classmate, Princess, is sitting next to me, and I ask her if her daddy would let her go to the movies this weekend. She said that he would. I'm thinking to myself that I have a date with two baby cowboys, a Princess, and the king of rocking roll. I feel as though I have died and gone to heaven and I'm only seven. First graders are done for today. All the kids rush to leave.

I go right across the street to my mama's house. My heart is beating fast with excitement. I sit myself down until I feel calm. I think to myself that I have a problem. I am pony-crazy. I feel like a race horse. I get my gear, jump on my bike and off I go. It's early and I can scout and still have time to get back to the rooming house to catch the race trackers. I pass my aunt's house. I take a fast right turn behind the shopping center, through the Hobo Trail, across the creek and over the bridge. I'm on the train tracks, down the hill, and onto the creek bed. So as not to get caught in traffic, I ride the creek bed under the bridge until I head back up toward the train tracks. I ride past the country store. I don't have money for apples or carrots, so I keep going. I pass the first horse pasture. Now I am almost to the second pasture. I look far ahead and I see horses very near. I'm here! I hide my bike and ease my way under the wire. The horses do not move. It's as if they have been waiting for me to come and play. I catch the first pony that's near. I string rope his neck and I grab a big chunk of mane. Then I jump the pony. We walk easy, in big circles. I ride awhile and then get off the horse and see how many other horses I can touch. I don't have much time. I only see seven horses that are close to me. I take the rope from my pony, and walk slowly to the horses. I was able to touch six of the seven horses. Only one pony ran. Now I must run to my bike and see if the other horses are near the fence. I don't see any horses and I don't have any more time to pony scout today. *There are two barns, each with forty thoroughbred race horses, just waiting for me.* I'm on a mission and I need to ride fast- those old cowboys don't mess around. They are always on time and I don't want to be left behind. It's too far to ride my bike. When I get one block from the rooming house, I see the cowboys walking to the car. I yell very loudly, "Cowboys!" and they see me. I've made it back just in time. I jump from my bike, still in motion. It parks itself in the bush as I jump into the car. Off we go for the three o'clock feeding- my very first! What a thrill! I pick the stalls and make sure all the manure is removed. I mop all wet spots and fill all the water buckets. The cowboys feed because they will give medication and special food to the race horses. That's what shepherds do; they take care of the pony. The boss yells to us that it's time to load up, and back home we go. It's over, just like that. We cowboy update as we ride. When we get home, I sit with the boys awhile, on the steps of the rooming house. As we restart our cowboy updates, my aunt comes over to say hello to the boys. She tells me to go and eat. I say bye to the boys and thank them for taking me to work with them. My aunt gets back from her walk around the circle. She has happy eyes when I tell her I am going to stay the night. I rush home and Cleopatra knows I'm not home to stay. She kisses me, and helps me get my things together. She tells me to be a good boy, and off I go, back to my aunt's house. I do my homework and my aunt checks it over. Now I sleep.

I hear cowboys going to work the next morning, but I have to go to school in four hours, so I fall back to sleep. My aunt wakes me up at seven o'clock. I have been dreaming of the time when I caught my first loose horse on the track when I was five-years-old. I've got to pay attention. I'm running late. I get dressed and get my homework. Now I'm ready. I'm going to walk with the new kids from the circle to school today. My little friend who died in the rooming house fire has a sister who goes to my school. Today, I will walk her to school. I see some kids coming toward me. There she is. We say hello, and we walk and talk. Some more of the kids run to meet us. The school is only ten blocks away. We're there in no time. The school bell is ringing, so we all run to class as we say goodbye to one another. The teacher says good morning, as Princess sits down next to me. She passes me a note. The note reads, *My daddy said Yes.* We flash a glance and a smile. I look to the back of the class at my baby cowboy classmate. I give him the thumbs up. He knows that's baby cowboy code talk for, "We're going to see the King and Princess this weekend!" The teacher tells me to pay attention. We are very busy this morning and there are two new kids coming into our class. The teacher reads their paper work and introduces the kids to us. They sit in the last two empty chairs in the classroom. The teacher calls for me to pass the new kids their school books. They have very happy eyes when they get their new books.

The teacher tells everyone to take out their books and homework. We hear a strange sound. We don't know what it is. It sounds like a baby. It is a baby. All the kids and the teacher jump up from their seats when they see a little black and white kitty cat jump from one of my little girl classmate's lunch pail. There is pure action in the classroom! Kids are all over the place running to try and catch the cat. No one is going to catch that cat. A kid just left the room, and left the door open. The kitty is running down the hallway. All the kids follow to try and catch him. Kids from the other rooms hear lots of noise and action. Next thing I know, kids are coming out of their classes.

The lunch bell rings. We head to the lunchroom, but before we get there, we hear lots of noise. The kitty is in the lunchroom eating from a student's food tray. After a little while, the little girl comes in, and the cat goes right up to her feet. My classmate picks up the cat and my teacher takes them both to the main office. This is a very, very exciting day and it's only high noon. All the kids are having a blast. They love the action. I glance over at the teachers' lunch table, and they love it also. When the bell rings, we all go to the playground. I catch up to my baby cowboy classmate. He is thrilled about the Elvis show, and so am I.

Back in class, the teacher checks homework and the students look over their books. My little kitty cat classmate is back in the classroom after spending lunch and play time in the office, talking with the school boss lady about that little baby kitty. The kid's not talking, so I guess we'll never know the details. By the way, this was the first time I'd ever seen a cat. I like cats. The bell rings and school is out.

When I get home, my mama wants me to go to the wash house. That's good news. My mother helps me get the wash together, and off I go. It takes me back to Texas- walking for my aunt and uncle to pick up and drop off lots of bags of garments from all over town. I get to the wash house and get the wash started.

Next, I go to the store, and Princess and her father are there. Her father tells me he will drop Princess off at the movies around one o'clock. "Nice to meet you, John Wayne." "Nice to meet you, too, sir." I'm thrilled! I get in the check out line and I have no money. I've lost the money. I tell the lady that I'll be right back. I walk to the door, and as I look down, I see the ten dollar bill my aunt gave me. I pick it up and rush back to the check-out lady. I pay, and run home with the items. I give the bag to my aunt, along with her change. Now, I must check the wash. It's ready to dry. I throw the wash into the dryer and rush back home. I tell my aunt that I'm going to go talk to the old cowboys. I get my guitar and I go. Everyone is home, so I put on a little show. I sing *The Lord Loves Me* on my guitar. They loved it. They yelled, "More, more, we want more!" I tell them I've got a date with my two little White baby cowboys, a little Black baby cowboy, a Princess, and a king called Elvis. "Do you know Elvis?" I asked the cowboys. "No, kid. We don't know him. We do know the King Brothers who are blues guitar players and great singers. When we see you again we will tell you about the Kings we know. Now, go and get your wash. Have a wonderful time at the Elvis-the-king show." "Thank you, boys. Goodnight." I rush back with my guitar. I kiss my aunt, and off I go. I get my bike, and when I get to the wash house, the owner is inside cleaning up the place. We talk, as I fold and bag the wash. The owner and his wife live upstairs, and we have known one another since I was a kid. They are very nice white people. I finish and tell him goodnight. As I ride away on my bike with the big bag on my handle bars, I think about the owner. He only has one arm, but he works as if he has both arms. I get home fast. Cleopatra is sitting out front. It's dark, and she's drinking a beer and smoking. She is happy that I made it back so fast. I take the big bag inside, then go back outside to sit with Cleo. My mama tells me she loves me and that I should go to sleep. The other kids are already sleeping. When my mother comes inside, I'm asleep on the sofa. When I wake up the next morning, I don't remember how I got in my bed. My mother calls for us to eat. When we finish, I take the kids to the sitter's house and then I go down the street to look for Princess. I see her and her little sister coming from their house. She is glad I am going to walk her to school, but first, we take her sister one street over to their friend's house. After we drop the baby sister off, we head to school. We talk of Elvis, and she is very excited about the show. She says that she is going to bring her friend from another school along with us to the movie house. She is so happy that her daddy said, "Yes."

Later in the day during lunch, I get the leftover apples and carrots.

There aren't many apples but the kids have given me lots of carrots for the horses. The kids think that I must be feeding all of the rabbits in town. I can't let any of the kids know about the horses, because they will try to follow the baby cowboy and me after school. We always take the dogs so that no one will have a clue that we are really scouting for horses- that don't belong to us. We are trespassers, and I do feel bad about that fact. But, what is a kid supposed to do? There are no black people with a pony in my town. If there are, I don't know them. I do know that the white people have lots of horses and lots of land. I've only seen one man while pony scouting. Unless he has a gun, I don't think he can catch me. I can run fast like a race horse. So, I think I'll take my chances. I can count well, and I count twenty-two horses that I have scouted so far. The bell rings and we go out to play. I want to talk to my baby cowboy classmate. Maybe he can go pony scouting with me after school. I'm going after class today with or without him. I am on a mission. I want to smell horse manure! I want to hear the sound of hooves pounding the ground! I want to see a pony running, bucking and kicking up dirt and making lots of dust! The school bell rings. When we take our seats, the teacher rearranges the chairs. My little classmate with the kitty cat is now sitting next to me. I ask her how her cat is doing. She say's the kitty is fine, and that when she was walking to school, the little cat was sitting in the road. She didn't want the cars to run over and kill the cat. So, she picked the cat up and put him in her lunch pail. As she tells me this story, the teacher tells me to pay attention. I'm thinking to myself that it's going to be much harder to pay attention, now that I'm sitting between two girls.

The bell rings and school is out for the weekend. My cowboy classmate can't go scouting with me today because he has chores. But, he will be coming to the big show tomorrow. I rush home. I'm on a mission. I get my gear. *I'm out of here!* Off I go, down the hill, behind my house and through the woods. I'm on the main highway. I ride fast past the store and down the hill, behind the gas station. I don't stop this time. I must slow down a little bit, because it rained last night and the trail is slick with mud. If I'm going to get hurt, let me get hurt on a pony- not a bike.

I jump off my bike and walk down the hill, trying not to fall. I see a pony. There's got to be more. I hide my bike. I only bring two carrots inside the wire fence. I walk right up to the pony. I've never seen him before. I rope the pony and tie him to the tree. I climb to the top of the tallest tree that's near. I can see the main gate. No one is here but me. If I stay here, close to my bike, I think I can ride in peace. I can hear if someone comes to the gate. I see more horses but they are much too far away. There is no tree I can hide behind, if someone comes out here. So, I play it safe. I climb down and give the pony a carrot. Then I jump the pony and we ride up and down the fence, near the woods and my bike.

What a fine pony he is! I wish he were mine. I jump off, and he gets the last carrot that I have in my pocket. I pet the pony on his head and turn him loose. *Whoa! Look at him go!* He's running, jumping, bucking and kicking up lots of trail dust! He's going back to the herd. I see lots of tracks. There are more horse shoes than hoof prints. Maybe most of these horses are not wild. I'm under the wire and on my bike. Off I go- just like a thoroughbred race horse. I want to take the short cut, but since it rained last night, the creek is too high for me to cross. I'm just a kid, so I play it safe, and take the long way around to my house. I'm there in no time. *What a ride! Thank you, Lord, for another great day in the life of a baby cowboy!*

I burst through the front door like a horse kicking on the stall wall of the barn. Everyone yells, "The baby cowboy is home, mama!" I walk in and my mother has a cake with candles on the table. With happy eyes, they sing *Happy Birthday* to me. It's my birthday, and I did not have a clue! What a thrill! I'm eight-years-old, as of one second after midnight last night. We eat dinner, and I make a wish and blow out the candles. My mother gives me a new pair of cowboy boots. My mother and my sisters give me a hug and a kiss. "Mama, I'm going with those cowboys in the morning." She tells me that my things are packed for the weekend. "See you, baby cowboy," they say as I walk out the door. I get my bike and off to my aunt's house I go. When I open the door, everyone yells, "Happy birthday, kid!" Five cowboys and my aunt are sitting at the table eating dinner. "I'm going with you cowboys in the morning!" "We thought you might, cowboy." I ask where the rest of the cowboys are. They tell me that they are shopping because today is pay day. After the cowboys go home, my aunt tells me that Rex and Billy Bob have called to talk to me. I call them back. Rex answers the phone and tells me that they are going to be at the movie house at one o'clock. They will pick me up at noon tomorrow. The baby cowboys are very excited, and so am I! I hug and kiss my aunt good night, and I'm fast asleep in no time.

Three o'clock comes early. I'm up and outside, waiting for the boys. I hear them and then I see them. I run to the car and off we go. When we get to the track, as soon as we are in the barn, the lights turn on and lots of cowboy race trackers jump from everywhere, as they yell, "Happy birthday, John Wayne! Good to see you! We love you, kid!" "Thank you, boys! I love you back! Now let's feed some race horses!" They tell me to wait, because they have something for me. One of the boys comes out of the stall leading a big white horse that is an ex-race horse. The big boss yells, "He's yours, kid! You ride him every day that you are here! Happy birthday, baby cowboy!" I am a happy boy. I rush to get the feed cart as the men load the feed and hay. I clean and fill the water buckets. There is nonstop action all morning. I sure miss coming here every day, but I have to go to school. The boss tells me to go easy today because it's my birthday. "When you finish the water buckets, saddle your new pony and ride around these two barns. Get the feel of that pony, because next week I'm going to let you ride on the racetrack!" When we saddle the pony, the boys give me a leg up, just like they do the real jockeys. I ride inside the barn before taking the pony to the door. What a horse! All of the boys are watching with very happy eyes. The boss leads me outside, and looks on as I ride. All the boys in the next three barns see me and yell, "Happy birthday, kid!" "Thanks!" I yell back at them. As I ride, I think of Big White, the first pony I ever rode. Now, I'm aboard another big white pony. I think of the sweet little old lady cowgirls and how they must be looking down from cowgirl heaven with very happy eyes and hearts. *Thank you, cowgirls. I love you. I'm sure you must know that it's my birthday. I just found out!*

The boss yells to me that it's time to go. I unsaddle and brush down my new pony. Well, he is not really mine, but he is mine when I'm here. That's wonderful. I'm not in a dream; this has really happened. And, I'm really paying attention- much more than I do in class. I say goodbye to the cowboys, until next time. They all yell back, as we drive slow and easy through the track parking lot, "Happy birthday, baby cowboy! We know you're going to the big Elvis show! Have a good time!" "I'm sure I will!" I yell back to them. We get home about nine o'clock. I take a bath and go to sleep.

I'm dreaming of riding a pony in the lake when I feel a shake on my arm. It's my aunt, and it's time for me to get ready for the show. When Rex and Billy Bob arrive, I kiss my aunt and she tells me to have fun. Off we go to the Elvis show. Billy Bob's daddy stops about a block from the movie house so we boys could walk and talk. Just before we get out of the car, the boys and Billy Bob's daddy yell, "Happy birthday, John Wayne! We love you!" *This is special.* "How did you boys know it was my birthday?" "Your aunt told us when we called for you yesterday." "Well boys, welcome to the party! Yesterday was when I found out, too. Now look here, boys, I'm eight, and let's not be late!" We jump from the car. We can see people in line for two blocks. We say bye to Billy Bob's father and off we go. I tell the boys that two of my classmates are meeting us, and I want to find them. They are very excited at the thought of meeting my friends. We walk easy down the line. "Hey boys, there's Princess!" She sees me and walks to me with her girlfriend. Now my classmate, the baby cowboy is here. We all introduce ourselves. Rex and Billy Bob are really checking things out. This is the first time in their young lives that they have seen this many Black kids in one location. Rex now has four Black kids at his school- one of them lives next door to him. Now, this is the year 1960, in Arkansas- deep in the south. And, this is the first time these boys have ever been to the mixed movie show. The boys have only been to the all-White movie house. There, you can sit anywhere you please. They don't know it yet, but we can't sit together. And, I don't know what to say. How do I tell my pals that we cannot sit together in the movie house? The movie house people separate the White kids into one line, and the Black kids in another line. We start to walk in, when Billy Bob and Rex realize that we are not going to sit together. I see no more happiness in their eyes. The boys are very upset. They cross into the Black line and say to me, "We want to sit together with you, cowboy, but the movie house people say we can't. So, we are not going inside. We have already seen this movie three times. We just thought it would be great to share the movie with you. Now you and your friends go, and we will wait for you after the show. Our parents are coming because we are having a surprise birthday party for you after the show." Rex and Billy Bob went to the back of the Black line and gave their tickets away to some little Black kids who didn't have a ticket or money. They were just some kids hanging around, hoping to see the show. They were thrilled and they thanked the boys with happy eyes. The Elvis movie will be very exciting and lots of fun. I'm glad to be here. *Thank you, Lord.* I understand why my little White baby cowboys would not go inside, but they don't realize how much I want to see the king of rocking roll. I've only had one chance to see the show. My pals Rex and Billy Bob understand that. At this point, I don't care about Integration, Desegregation, the Proclamation, or the Damn Nation! I'm going to see a Sensation called Elvis- the King of Rock and Roll!

We go inside, and when the movie starts, all the kids go crazy. We are all jumping around in our seats. The place is going wild! I'm thinking about my pals outside. Princess and her girlfriend sit between me and the baby cowboy. They have never seen Elvis before, and they are having the time of their young lives. I stand up and look down into the White section. They are out of their seats with joy. I go and get popcorn, and look from the lobby windows onto the street, hoping to see my pals outside. I couldn't see them, so I go back to the top floor and eat popcorn with my friends. They filled me in on the parts I missed. The kids are very nice. No one is throwing popcorn, or sodas, or trash down over the rail into the White section. No one is name-calling. The kids just want to have fun. I'm glad to be here. I wish my baby cowboys, Rex and Billy Bob were here, but I understand why they left. The kids are now dancing all over the place! Elvis is playing his guitar and singing. Some girls downstairs are passing out on the floor. I look and Princess, and ask her if she and her friend are going to pass out. "No," she answers with happy eyes. For some reason the music is getting very loud and the kids are loving it. At this point, the kids are dancing in the narrow space between the seats. Girls are really crying and bawling with tears dropping down their faces. I see pure pandemonium. But, no one is confused, for we kids have just witnessed a sensational show! They call him *the King of Rock and Roll*, and his name is

Elvis. There is a whole lot of rocking and moving going on. I get my friends and we start to leave slowly, so as not to get trampled, or get caught up in a baby stampede. Everything is fine, and we are in the lobby and out the door before all the kids come running out. What a great time all the kids had today!

I see my pals coming down the street with happy eyes. They can see we had a great time. They say to me, "John Wayne, bring your friends three doors down to the restaurant on the corner!" Here comes the father of Princess. I invite him to the party, too. We all walk down the block. When we get inside the place, I see my sister going to the little girls' room. She wishes me a happy birthday again. At that point I knew, or thought I knew, what was to come. *Wow!* There's Cleopatra with the babies, my aunt, and one dozen fabulous cowboy race trackers. There's Rex, Billy Bob and his parents, the girlfriend of Princess, and my baby cowboy classmate. What a great time everyone is having! They are talking, eating and dancing. This is my first time here. My mother works here part-time. So, I'm sure to come back. The parents tell me later that day, that Rex and Billy Bob paid for my entire party. I don't know what to say on a blessed day, except, "Thank you, Lord." I thanked my pals and I thanked their parents for not trying to talk the boys out of having such a party. "Any time, John Wayne. Peace." I'm thinking to myself that these are some very special baby cowboys. We all slowly start to leave. Everyone had a great time. We all say goodnight. Princess and her father take the baby cowboy home, along with the other girl. Billy Bob and his parents take my mother and her kids home. Rex and his parents take my aunt and me home. The race trackers all have rides. What a legendary day in the life of a baby cowboy. When I get home, I get my guitar and play awhile before I fall asleep thinking of Elvis- not horses. But, I'm sure that before the night is over, I'll be dreaming of a pony somewhere, that needs a baby cowboy's touch.

I hear people talking. I look out the window. It's some of the cowboys coming home from a night out on the town. I raise up my window and yell, "I'm coming with you cowboys in the morning!" "We hope so! Bring your new saddle for your new pony!" I look at the clock. It's ten o'clock. I've got five hours to dream. I fall back to sleep. I'm up early- long before the chickens are up. I'm dressed and sitting on the front steps, playing my guitar until the cowboys are ready to go to the racetrack. I go and get my saddle and head out to the car. I'm sitting in the back seat on my new saddle with four cowboys sitting next to me. We boys cowboy update until we get to work. First thing we do when we arrive is feed and water the horses. I clean all the water buckets. While the horses are eating we all clean stalls. We wrap legs with big white strips of cotton. It's good for the horses. We brush and groom them and we saddle up the horses. When they finish eating, we put bits in their mouths. Next, we pick the hooves-

72

all four, every day. We walk the horses around the shed row- inside the barn. We take them outside to put them on the hot walking machine. The horses are walking, and we are still cleaning the entire barn. The pony boys are here. The jockeys are coming, also. The big boss calls for me. I run to his office and he says, "You're done for the day, kid. Get your saddle and go play with your pony until it's time to go home!"

I hurry back to the car. I get my saddle. My pony is ready. His stall is so clean that I could eat off its floor. His hooves are picked. He is groomed. All four legs are wrapped. He is a fabulous thoroughbred and an ex-race horse. I saddle him up. We walk down and around the shed row until the boss yells that it's time to go. Time flies when you're having fun! I unsaddle, and the pony boy tells me to just leave my pony in the stall. He has to go to work leading the race horses around the track.

I get my saddle and off we go. We say bye to all the boys. We head to the main gate, when suddenly we hit the brakes. We see men running across in front of us. "Loose horse!" they yell. We jump from the car. They tell me to stay by the car. The cowboys run behind the barns. There are lots of barns on the backside. A horse could get hurt. Sweet sounds of hooves are pounding the ground, "click-clack click-clack." I turn around, and the pony is almost standing between the car and the barn. I walk two feet. Oh, what a treat. He stands still and lets me catch him. I don't know where he lives, so we talk. Men come running from all sides of the barns. Someone yells, "The kid's got the pony!" They pass the word through the backside. The owner, the trainer and the groom of the pony thanked me with happy eyes. They tell us they have just pulled into town from Texas. They take the horse and go. We go out the main gate bound for home. "Thank you, John Wayne, for another fine job this morning." "Thank you, cowboys!" They tell me to have a good day in school tomorrow, as they go inside the rooming house. I have to go to school tomorrow and try to pay attention. It's not going to be easy- I'll be sitting between two girls, and thinking of this wonderful weekend.]

CHAPTER EIGHT

School's out for now for a two-week vacation. Cleo and the kids are going to Texas to see her aunt and uncle. My aunt and I are not going because we will go this summer. That only means one thing- I'll be going to the race track every day. I run home. My mother and the kids are packing for the trip. Tomorrow they will catch the train to Texas to where my mother was born. She is so excited, because she knows this vacation is just what the doctor ordered. I pack some of my things to take to my aunt's house. I hug and kiss my sisters, my brother and my mama. Off I go to my aunt's house. She's not home, so I play my guitar for awhile. I want to see the cowboy race trackers, but I look out of the window and I don't see their car. My aunt is coming down the street with bags in both arms, so I run to help her. She has been downtown most of the day. She's glad to see me, and happy that I'm going to be at her house for two weeks. She tells me that she needs me to help her around the houses tomorrow after I come back from the track. We eat supper. I see the boys are home, so I go over to say hello. I let them know I'm going with them tomorrow. "Yes, John Wayne, we thought you would. Glad to have you, kid," they all say to me. Out the door I go. I walk easy down the sidewalk around the circle. As I pass where the sweet little old lady cowgirls once lived, I think of them, and I miss them. I begin to feel very, very sad. I tear up. I stop and sit down on the last step at the last cowgirl's house. I stare at a big *For Sale* sign in the front yard, and that's when it hits me, hard. The flood gates open and I cry like a baby. As I wipe my eyes with the back of my hand, I stand and walk around the rest of the circle. All the cowgirls are in heaven, and I've got no more sweet old ladies to talk with. They are all gone to greener pasture. I go inside, and fall asleep.

The next day, I'm working on the racetrack with some old Black, legendary wild horse wranglers. There are middle-aged wranglers from the Continent of Africa. The three boys are very nice, but don't talk much. Today is special. When they were my age, the cowboys tell me, they were riding most of the four-legged creatures of the jungle. This included what they called the "stripe-pony" known as the zebra. The three wranglers also say that this will be their last rendezvous- they will be going back home. "We enjoyed you very much, John Wayne Jay." I met these guys last year. They didn't speak much English. But, now they speak well enough to pronounce my name correctly. I thank them for blessing me with their presence. The boss calls for me to saddle up my pony. I'm going to ride the track- my first time ever on a big time thoroughbred racetrack! I'm being lead around by my boss on a big white ex-race horse. What a wonderful adventure in the life of a baby cowboy! I also have my Texas saddle and my new cowboy boots. It's very cold this morning. We had a very light workout for the horses. That's why my boss could take me around the track; most of the horses were hot walked in the barn and on the walking machine. There were only two other horses besides mine on the track. Christmas is coming soon, and the track will be full of horses during the first of the year. The morning passes fast- like a race horse.

I'm home, and now I have to go through the Hobo Trail. It's the short cut to the train station. My mama and the kids are leaving soon. I want to see them off. I see them standing out front. I hug and kiss them all and tell them to have a great time in the Lone Star State. Cleopatra puts money in my pocket as she kisses me one last time, and tells me to be a good boy. "I love you," she says. "I love you, too, mama." And off they go. The train is moving. My sisters are looking at me from the window. They wave as the train slowly pulls away from the station. I stand on the platform until the train is out of sight. I jump down on the tracks and start walking home. When I get to the bridge, I see hobos coming and going. There are two hobos having a fight over a bottle of wine. They are both rolling down the hill near the creek. So, I sit on the big rock at the top of the trail. I've got a ringside seat. One of the men is now in the water and he's trying to get out, but he can't. The other man is holding him down. Suddenly, they are both in the cold creek water. Somehow, they are still holding on to the side of the creek bed. At that point I spring into action. A white hobo man put me on my first horse ever. I run down the hill near the men. I look around on the ground, and find a long tree branch shaped like a fishing hook. I drag the hook branch to the edge of the water. There's a small tree, so I hook the tree, and there is enough branch left to reach the men. They catch hold of the branch and slowly pull themselves up and out, onto the creek bed. They are in a state of shock. They are sucking for air as they say, "Thanks, kid! You have just saved the lives of two hobos!" We walk slow and easy up the hill to the middle of the trail. "Why are you men fighting?" Neither of them said a word. I saw the broken bottle in the bush. They had very sad eyes. Cleopatra had given me money at the train station. I don't know how much, because I have not yet looked. So, I give them five dollars for food and drinks- on the condition that they agree not to fight anymore. They look at me with happy eyes and say, "We love you, kid." "Peace." Off I go, through the remaining parts of the Hobo Trail, into the shopping center parking lot, and across the street to the house.

My aunt and I cowboy update a bit. The phone rings. It's the Guitar Man, Abner Wingate Jay- my daddy. He is glad to know I am doing well and that my sisters and mother are fine, too. I tell him everyone is in Texas except my aunt and me. He tells me to put my aunt on the line. She and Abner talk for awhile before they say goodbye. My aunt tells me that my daddy wants to come and get us and take us back to Georgia. I thought about the prospects of going back, but I did not see a lot of horses in Georgia. I don't think there is a racetrack in the town. Although, I do recall seeing a couple of people on horseback.

The next morning, I am looking forward to another adventure. It's cold this morning. As we drive to the track, the cowboys are saying we might get snow today or tomorrow. I love snow. And I'd like to ride a pony in the snow. There is lots of action as we pull into the main gate. Many horses are being unloaded all over the backside. I have never seen this many horses in my life! We hurry to the barn and start the feeding process, which is a very happy time for the horses. All the boys are working together. I can see it's going to be a busy day. As the morning progresses, the barn is clean and all the horses have gone to the track. We have just a few more little chores to do before the horses come back from their morning workout. Then, we give them a bath. After hot walking awhile, we bed them down proper- with clean, dry and fluffed stalls, fresh clean water, feed, and lots of hay. That's it for today. I didn't ride my pony horse this morning, because on busy days he has to work, leading race horses around the track for their morning workout.

I go home and my aunt tells me that Rex and Billy Bob called, and want to get together. I take a bath, eat and go to sleep for a few hours. When I wake up the baby cowboys are calling. They want to pick me up tomorrow when I finish working at the racetrack.

My aunt and I decide to take a walk downtown and go window shopping. It's late, and the stores are closed for the day. As we walked, something really caught my eye. I have picked up dolls for my sisters in the past. They have little white baby dolls. They also have Spanish dolls, and the last time I was window shopping, I found a very rare China doll. As I recall, my sisters went wild with joy. They loved her. She was the first China doll they had seen. They played with her every day. Now, what really caught my eye, was the first black baby doll I had ever seen. She was standing in the window between the white dolls and the other dolls. I called to my aunt as she was walking ahead of me. She walked back to see what was in the window. She told me to come back early the next morning and buy the dolls for my sisters. As we headed back home, my aunt and I walked down through town the long way home, because it was too dark to go into the Hobo Trail.

When I get home, I go over to see the cowboys. I tell them I won't be able to go with them in the morning, because I have to buy my sisters a new black baby doll- the first black baby doll I've ever seen. I want to be the first person in the store. "Now boys, I can be ready for the afternoon feeding." "That's good, John Wayne. You go shopping and get those dolls, and we will pick you up at three o'clock."

My aunt has gone to sleep. I should be sleeping also, but I can't. So, I play my guitar. Before long, I hear the police and the fire trucks. I jump up and look out the window. The three-story rooming house across the street is on fire. I run outside and stand on the sidewalk. The fire is not bad. It's on the first-floor and it's only one room that caught fire. "Help me, sonny," I hear. There are some very old people who need help down the stairs. At this point there's only one fire truck here. So, I run across the street. I go in the back door of the house, and I'm able to walk three sweet little old white ladies out of the very dark and smoky rooming house. I walk them back across the street to my house. I sat them on the front steps and went inside to get cups of water and cookies for the girls. More fire trucks are arriving. All of the people are safe and are in the shopping center parking lot across the street. My aunt is out front talking with the ladies. After a few hours the firemen let the tenants back in.

The ladies hug and kiss me and say to me, "Thank you, baby cowboy. You must be an angel. We're sure that you are. We have known you since you were a little baby cowboy running up and down the sidewalk, "click-clack, click-clack," on your stick horses with beer cans pressed around the heels of your feet as horse shoes. Over the years, we girls have called you some very bad names because we just couldn't believe that you would be up so early, or out so late at night on your stick pony making all that noise! "Click-clack! Click-clack," we are old ladies, for God's sake! We go to bed early and we get up late. We sure made a very bad mistake and we're very sorry. We love you, John Wayne. We didn't talk to your old cowgirl friends very much over the years, but we do know how much you helped those old ladies. And they loved you. We know you miss them. We look out the window sometimes and see you walking and looking, slow and easy, at the houses in the circle where they once lived. Now, sonny boy, we remember when you were working for our landlords, the husband and the wife, selling fruits and vegetables out in the country. You were just a little cowboy. Those dozen little old black ladies are in heaven. There are more than a dozen sweet old white ladies living right here in this three-story rooming house, and we need you. You can be our baby cowboy; someone to talk to, go shopping for us and help us with small chores." "All right, ladies. I'm sold. You're going to make me cry. Now go home girls, and I'll come by tomorrow."

The street is back to normal. Everyone is back in their rooms. All except the man whose room caught on fire. He has to go get checked out but he should be fine. The girls get to the front door and just before they go inside, they turn to me and say, "Sonny boy, we saw you ride stick horses and we saw you ride a real horse. When we lived on the top floor a few years ago, we could look over into the horse pasture and see the hobo put you on the back of that big white horse and lead you around. One last thing before we go to sleep, sonny, we remember when you rode the Great Dane dog right down the sidewalk in front of the house between the fruit and vegetable stand. Goodnight, cowboy." "Goodnight, ladies." *Thank you Lord, that no one was hurt.*

I go in the house and my aunt says to me, "Young fellow, I have been here for twenty years and those ladies have never said more than two words to me. Now they all love you and they want to be your friend. They are going to be your new cowgirl replacements. I think it's wonderful because I would always speak to those old ladies as I would walk up and down the sidewalk in front of their house. But, they would never speak to me. They just looked at me with not so happy eyes. Now, it looks like we may be the best of friends." Lord, what a great day in the life of a baby cowboy. I hug and kiss my aunt, and off to sleep I go.

I hear the cowboys going to work. I watch from the window as the boys leave, knowing very well that I will be going to the track this afternoon. I fall back to sleep. When daylight comes, I'm up and dressed. The stores don't open for two more hours, but I'm going downtown right now. I can window shop some more. I'm walking through the Hobo Trail. No one is fighting. There are just a few hobos sleeping in the bush. I pass slow and easy so as not to wake the boys, when suddenly I hear, "Hey, kid!" It was one of the hobos who was fighting. He said hello and thanked me again for being such a brave little kid. "You saved me and my friend because we were too drunk to help ourselves." Then he gave me a candy bar. "Thank you, sir. Why do you boys drink that stuff if it makes you fight and push one another down the hill into the cold creek water?" "It's a long story, kid. Maybe one day I'll be able to say, but right now I don't have the time. See you, kid. Take care of yourself." I walked down a little way over the bridge, jumped onto the railroad tracks and walked to town- all the while eating my candy bar. I stop at the music store. There are lots of nice guitars on display in the window. I see one that looks just like one of my guitars. I walk down to the store where the dolls are. It looks to be a busy day in the downtown area. The shop owners are coming from the parking lots with keys in hand. I buy a bag of mixed nuts from the newsstand and I feed the birds, until all of the shops are open. The first moment I see people inside the store with the dolls, I run to stand next to the door. I want to be first in line. I'm thinking about how happy my sisters will be to see the new dolls! The store opens. I go inside to the toy section, and there are no black baby dolls that I can see. So I walk around the store, and I look in the back of the window display. The black doll has fallen down on the floor and no one can see her. I go to the counter and ask to buy two black baby dolls, and the young lady goes in the back, and comes out with two dolls. I tell her that the black doll in the window has fallen. I pay for the dolls and off I go. When I get home, I tell my aunt that one more doll is what I need. She gives me enough money for three. This time I ride my bike very fast. When I get there, the lady says that they only have one doll left. So, I ask to buy the doll that fell. I pay and thank the lady, and ride my bike home. I am thinking of my friend, who died in the fire. His little sister lives in the back of the circle. I'm going to give her this beautiful, black baby doll.

The cowboys are back. I see them as I look through the window of my room. I'm up and outside when the race trackers walk out to the car. We say hello, and the boys say to go get my saddle. "The big boss is off today, but he left word that you can ride your pony after work, while we do some extra leg work on a pony who was hurt this morning." I get my saddle and off we go. They are happy that I have some new, little old lady cowgirls in the circle again. This time, I'm blessed with more cowgirls than before.

When we get to the track, we feed right away. In the afternoons, I fill all the water buckets in one barn only. But, in the mornings I fill the water buckets in two barns. That's 80 water buckets that I clean, then fill with fresh water, so that the horses can stay happy and in good health. The cowboys are just about finished with the stalls. They are picked up and dry, with three feet of straw, and a big hay bag hanging right outside each stall door. And the barn smells good. The cowboys run to put my pony outside on the hot walking machine. He walks for half an hour before I saddle him. We ride around only the outside of the three barns, as the backside is getting packed with race horses coming into town for the opening day. Before I unsaddle my pony, a man walks up to me and says, "Sonny, I broke and trained that pony you're sitting aboard. I also trained his mother and his father. My name is Doug. What's yours, kid?" "My name is Cellulose John Wayne Jay." He said my pony is from California. He is glad that I have a chance to ride him this year. I thanked him, and told him he did a very good job training this pony. "See you around, kid." I head back to the barn and bed my pony down proper. And off we go.

When I get home, my aunt and I eat and cowboy update until I fall asleep. I dreamed of Texas wild mustangs. I'll be there this summer. My mama called to wake me up at three o'clock in the morning. Oh, what a happy day. We talk just a little while before I have to get dressed. I don't need my saddle, because my pony will work on the racetrack today. I rush out and jump in the car with the cowboys. We are always thrilled to see one another. They tell me that they are going to be really busy today, so they want me to just watch most of the day. "We have new horses coming in from California. There'll be lots of action this morning, kid. Let's stay safe. Stay alert and pay attention to details. Understand?" "Yes." I replied.

Once we get to the barns we know what to do. I get started with fresh water in both barns. I'm hoping to see the new horses this morning. The boys tell me we're going to have half of the next barn. That means we may have lots of horses coming in all week, from all around the nation. The jockeys are arriving, and the pony boys are arriving, also. I get a chance to cowboy update with them- they're early to our barn. They know me from when I was a little baby cowboy and I caught my first loose horse on the backside of the racetrack. They are glad to see me. The horses are ready. I leg up one of the jockeys and he tells me not to lift him too high. As they can see, I have grown and I am stronger. I am going to go up to the track and watch through the fence to check out all the new horses. Some are first time starters. Action is happening all morning long. There's a rider down on the ground, and the horse is running around, until the pony boy catches up to the race horse. The horse is all right and feeling good. The jockey is not doing so well, though. He is still down. Lots of people run to help him. I don't think he will be able to ride anymore today. They carry him off of the track. I'm sure he must need to see the doctor. Meanwhile, training gets back underway and all the horses are looking great. Some of the young horses are getting starter-gate tested. The boys yell from the barn, "It's time to go, kid!"

When I get home, I run inside and get cleaned up. My aunt is not home, so I get something to eat and then change my guitar strings. I know that I'm going to play a song today for my new cowgirls. They should be up and around- it's almost noon. I don't want to be too early, because the ladies told me that they sleep late. I see them sitting out on the front porch. I walk over with my guitar and say hello. The girls are glad to see me. They ask me to play something. I play the only full song that I know. That is, *The Lord Loves Me, Yes I Know, for the Bible Tells Me So.* I start to play and sing. The men and the rest of the little old white ladies come down from their rooms to say hello and hear me play. When I finished, the ladies and the five old men clapped and yelled for more. I asked if they needed anything from the store. "Yes, we do, sonny boy. Can you read?" "Yes, ma'am. I can read." "Well then, we will write a list of the items we need." I play until the ladies get the notes and the money. There are sixteen ladies in the house, and nine of them give me notes and money. I can see that this is going to take awhile. I am so happy to help these people for they are blessed. The big old house they live in is made of wood. The entire house could have burned down very easily. My aunt told me that one of the men in the house was smoking and drinking in bed, and fell off to sleep. I'm in the store and I am going to need a push cart. I never needed a cart when I shopped for my sweet little old cowgirls. They never really needed much. My new cowgirls had put their names on each note, so as not to have a mix-up. I stack the items with the notes in the cart. The check-out lady knows me, and she bags the items in order. I thanked her, as I paid and left the store. When walking back across the street, I look ahead, and one of the little old ladies is playing my guitar. As I get closer, she sounds very good. They see me coming across the street, pushing the shopping cart. They have very happy eyes. I have been in the store for almost one hour. I carry five big shopping bags up to the porch where everyone is sitting. They all thank me, and each of them give me a dime. The little lady playing my guitar tells me that my strings are turned upside down, so I must be left-handed. "Yes, ma'am." "Kid, would you sing that song again for us?" I begin to play my left-handed guitar, and the little old ladies join in and sing along. Two of the men share their strong, deep voices. It sounded very good. We are having a great time when my aunt yells, "The phone is for you! The baby cowboys are calling!" So, I say goodbye to everyone, and they tell me they love me, and that I can come back whenever I want. "You're our new little man." I ease my way down the long stairs to the sidewalk, and when I get the phone, the boys tell me to be ready in one hour.

My aunt and I cowboy update until Rex and Billy Bob arrive. She is so happy that I have lots of new little old lady cowgirls once again. The baby cowboys are here. I go outside and the boys get out of the car. They tell me to bring my saddle and my guitar, and off we go. When we get to the ranch, we run to the barn with my saddle and guitar. I am thrilled to be here once again with my pals! We get our horses from the stalls. The stalls have already been cleaned. The water is fresh. We groom the horses, saddle up, and off we go. Rex has some new trails for us to ride. We wave at the black kid next door. I have met him before. He's a nice kid, but he doesn't like horses. As we ride, the boys say they are doing well in school, but they are looking forward to summertime. We ride down through the woods, to the new trail. We cross the stream, and ride up and over the hill. Rex says his daddy is going to buy the next pasture ahead. He is also going to buy more race horses. As we ride, we see the boys from last time. They go to the same school as Rex, and they want to ride with us. They ride up to the gate. They unlock the gate and come in, and we five cowboys ride the new trail. What a wonderful place this is. The new kids tell us we can ride in their pasture the next time. The boys have ropes on their saddles. They tell us that they are team ropers. We are running out of daylight. We tell them goodbye, until we meet again.

As we head back, when crossing the stream, we see hogs. They are big razorback hogs. They are the biggest I've ever seen. They run as we get closer. When we get to the barn, we unsaddle and clean and brush the horses down. Then we bed them down proper. We give them clean water, feed, and lock the stall door. We stuff the hay bags hanging outside the door. We don't have three feet of straw, like they do on the racetrack.

We go inside and cowboy update with the parents. They are so happy that we are together. They want to hear me play my guitar, so I play the only song I know. Rex has a drum set. His mom says he is going to have to move the drum set out into the barn. Then he can really go wild and play as long as he wants to. Maybe one day we will play together in a rock and roll band, like Elvis. We say goodnight, and Rex carries my saddle to the car. We had a wonderful time. Now off we go, headed back to my house.

Cleopatra and the kids are coming home from Texas tomorrow. My aunt and I eat supper, and she says she has a new song for me. She plays the piano for me and sings the new song. I like it, but I also like to sleep. It's a big day tomorrow on the racetrack. We can work on that song later. We say goodnight and off to sleep I go.

I'm up very early. I sit on the front steps looking down the sidewalk to where the lady cowgirls once lived. Although they never talked to the white ladies, they must be thrilled, from heaven, knowing that I helped those ladies, and will always help them when I can. I see the cowboys coming so I run to the car, and off we go. When we get to the barn, the new cowboys are already feeding the horses. I start my chores, and the morning is off to a fast start. The backside is full. There are no more barns available. The jockeys and pony boys are walking into the barn. The horses are ready, and they are looking and feeling good. The boys are legged up, and to the track they go. Five horses are not working today, so we hot walk them in the barn. It's very cold today, and very hard walking on the outside hot walking machine. They say we may have snow tomorrow. I sure hope so. I love snow. I have never ridden a pony in the snow, but I would love to. The boss yells to us that it's time to go. He tells me to bring my saddle tomorrow. My pony won't be working, so I can ride.

When I get home, Cleopatra and the kids are sitting on the porch talking with my aunt. I hug and kiss them all, for I have missed them a great deal. I run to get the dolls for my sisters. They are thrilled! They have never seen a black baby doll. They have new dolls to play with now. My baby brother is crying. I guess he wants a doll also. He sees that I have one more doll left, and he wants it. I tell him that I will go to the store later and get him one. So, he stops crying. I give the last doll to my sisters and I tell them to go around the circle and give the doll to my dead friend's little sister. I'm sure she will be happy to have a new, black baby doll. I tell my sisters that she need not know that it's from me. They understand. They take my little brother along, and he gives the doll to the little girl. What a happy day. They all stay and play most of the day.

We are all eating supper as Cleopatra informs me that school starts tomorrow, and that I have to come home tonight. I run over and let the cowboys know that I have to go to school tomorrow and won't be able to go with them in the morning. They wish me well, and say that they will see me on the weekend.

The next morning I'm up early. I'm sitting on the back porch. It's cold and still dark outside. I love the dark. Everything is still. I can hear and think very clearly. I want to see snow early this morning. I cannot see, but I feel a light rain. I jump up and turn on the porch lights. Now I can see big snow flakes. I go back inside and get dressed. I play around in the front yard. The snow is really coming down hard. I have seen snow before, at my grandmother's house in Ohio- but not like this. The street and yard seem to have disappeared, and are now all white. My mother comes out and says she wants me or my sister to stay home and babysit the kids. She has to go to work early today. My sister wants to stay home and babysit. That is great news. I walk my mother half way to work. Then I go to school. There aren't many kids there, but it's still early. I hang around the school yard, playing in the snow. I see my classmate, the baby cowboy, coming into the school yard. We cowboy update until the bell rings. There are not many kids in class. The teacher comes in and tells us that there will be no school today. It is going to snow all day. I go to the playground, and play in the snow with some of the kids who are waiting on their parents. The snow is about two feet deep now. I'm glad I live across the street. I say goodbye to the kids, and I go home. Later that day, my sisters and brother and I make a big snowman. This is the first time we've ever played in snow this deep. It's going to get much deeper by tonight. We go next door. There are lots of kids to play with. I want to go pony scouting down behind the gas station, but the snow is up over my cowboy boots. I don't want to catch a cold and get sick. I walk over to my aunt's house. I put on my rain boots, and some new socks. My aunt needs me to shop and do some little chores. She tells me to take my time, and to go over and check on the cowgirls. No one's sitting on the porch today, so I knock on the door. A man opens the door and say's "Hello, sonny boy, I'll call the girls for you." All the ladies are glad to see me. Five ladies need me to go shopping. I wait for the shopping list and money from the sweet little old lady cowgirls. When they come back to the door, they bring me a cup of hot cocoa, along with the money and shopping list. I walk across the street and not many cars have passed by. I'm drinking my cocoa and thinking about the horses down by the train tracks. The wind is blowing hard, and the snow is still coming down. I could never make it to the pastures. It's hard just walking to the store. No pony scouting for me anytime soon. The snow is too deep. As I shop, I see kids from my school, with their parents. We talk for a few minutes about the big snow storm. Lots of people are now coming to the store. I rush to finish and get back across the street. There are lots of cars now driving up and down the roads. Big salt trucks are rolling, and spreading salt all around the town. The ladies are so glad to see me as I make it back, with everything intact. "Thank you, baby cowboy. We hoped and prayed that you would come by today." My aunt is so happy that I can help those ladies. I go over and cowboy update with the old cowboys. I tell them that I'm going with them in the morning if there is no school.

Later on, Cleopatra informs me that school has been cancelled for tomorrow. That's good news for me, because now I'm going to ride a pony in the snow! My mama knows that I want to go with the cowboys in the morning. So, she packs my gear, hugs and kisses me, and off I go back to my aunt's house. It's getting dark, and I only have ten blocks to walk. What a wonderful night. It snowed hard all day, but now the snowfall has stopped. I go inside and eat supper with my aunt.

The next morning, the track opens late, and there's lots of ice on the track. We hot walk most of the horses. My boss lets me ride the pony horse out back, behind the barn in the deep snow. This is my first pony ride in the snow! Tomorrow is opening day, and there are lots of people in town. I'll be in school, but maybe after school, I can see the big race. I say bye to the boys in the next barn. After tomorrow's race, some of them will be going to New Mexico. They tell me it's a big, wonderful place with lots of hills and valleys, and wild horses all over the country side. New Mexico is next to Texas, they tell me. I tell them I'd like to go there someday. I unsaddle my pony, brush him, and bed him down for the night. Then, off we go, back home. Another great day on the backside of the racetrack.

The next evening, I cowboy update with the old cowboys and they tell me that they will take me to see the last two races. Five horses will run from our barn. When they told me the names of the horses running, I felt as if they could win. So, the next day after class I rush to the rooming house. The boys are just about ready to go. When we get close to the race-track, we start looking for a place to park. This is a big day, and there are lots of cars everywhere. We push our way down to the starting gate. The horses are on the track. They look wonderful and happy. They are in the gate, and they're off! The pony from our barn is in second place and he's taking the lead early. He's a speed horse. I hope he can hold the lead. He's in very good shape and he knows this track. The lead is opening up- our pony is going to win by four lengths! What a great race! Some of the boys in the winner's circle are the grooms from the rooming house. I am really happy for those boys and the pony! The next and last race, our pony ran first and second. This is a great day for our barns! Later that night, after having supper with the boys, they tell me that the barns had four winners, and one second place on the day. Now, on the track, that's a great day! I say goodnight, and thank the boys for taking me along. I tell my aunt good night and that I'll be back tomorrow after school. When I get home, my mother is excited for me. She knows that I had a great time. Mother says school lets out at noon tomorrow. I do my homework and go to sleep.

Weeks and months pass, and school is out for summer. I'm going back to Texas. My aunt says we leave tomorrow. Rex and Billy Bob are in summer school, and they say that going to Texas would be better. They tell me to have a good time and that we will ride and swim when I return. "Peace."

I'm getting really excited about the mustang pony that I rode the last time I was in Texas. I hope he is still at the ranch. I walk around the circle one last time before I leave town. As I pass where the little old lady cowgirls once lived, they put a smile on my face. Though I don't see or hear them, I always feel as if they are with me. When I make the circle, I stop at my new cowgirls' house to let them know that I will be out of town for a few weeks. They have sad eyes, but are happy that I'm not going away for the whole summer. I tell them how much I'm going to miss them all. More girls are coming down stairs. "Hello! Hey, cowgirls! Let's have a party!" I run across the street and get my guitar. When I return, the ladies have cookies and soda pop. My friend has her guitar and we play and sing. They say that I'll be missed and to take care of myself. They tell me to please remember that the landlord's son will be needing me at the fruit stand for part of the summer. I'm thinking that this is great, because I'll have a chance to check the horses down behind the country fruit stand. "Bye, cowgirls!"

The next morning, my aunt and I take a cab to the train station. Cleo and the kids are there to see us off. I give them a hug and a kiss and off we go. I love trains. My last trip to Texas, I rode the bus. I'm sure I will see more countryside, and more horses and cows this time. My aunt and uncle pick us up at the train station. We are happy to see one another. It's raining now, but my uncle says it should stop by tonight. I'm going to work with my uncle tomorrow. It's going to be hot in the dry cleaners. I will have to make sure I drink lots of water. After supper, I go to sleep early.

The next morning when we get to work, my uncle's son, the Texas cowboy, is waiting in front of the shop. He is going to take me to the ranch this morning. No working in the hot shop today. I am going to ride a Texas mustang pony! The cowboy tells me that I've gotten much taller, and that he is happy to see me. We drive out to his friend's ranch. He and his son are out back in the barn, looking over some new horses. We are glad to see one another. The cowboys have a new barn. They have twenty stalls and will have lots of horses this summer. We take two trucks to the ranch, because the cowboy's son has to come back early. Tomorrow I will bring my saddle. The cowboys catch a pony for me to ride. What a wonderful looking pony he is! I get on him and he starts to walk sideways, and then he takes off fast. I slow him down in a circle. The cowboys yell, "Easy, John Wayne, that's a blind Texas mustang!." I rode him near the vegetable garden, and somehow he ended up stepping into a watermelon. We ride until it falls away from his feet. The boys thought that was funny. I like the pony. It was a very different ride because he's blind, and maybe he walks sideways so he doesn't hit things head-first. I take him back and unsaddle him. The boys say the pony was born blind. They found him wandering out in the countryside. No one ever claimed the pony. The police said that they could keep him until someone claims him. That was five years ago. No one ever rides the pony. I am going to be his new cowboy as long as I'm here in Texas. The son has to leave for work now. The cowboys saddle three horses, and we ride. We see that the fence is down, and some cows are out in the road. Once we get the cows, we fix the fence. Then we scout for Texas Long horns. The herd is just up ahead, and the cowboys are missing one cow. We ride most of the day searching, until we find the cow in the lake, taking as swim all by himself. We are glad to see that he is okay. After we get him back to the herd, we go home. The cowboys say we have to move cattle tomorrow, and that I should bring my saddle. My uncle is out of town, but my aunts are home. They want a cowboy update. We talk for hours. The food is ready, so I eat, take a bath and I go to sleep.

The cowboys are here early to get me. I'm already outside with my saddle when they drive up. "Howdy, baby cowboy!" "Hello, cowboys! Good to see you!" When we get near the ranch, we stop to eat. When we get to the ranch, the cows are in plain sight. That means that our job is going to be easy. We open the gate, and we run the cattle into the next pasture. We look around for the horses. The cowboys drive over the ridge and look around. We spot the horses. Once we saddle up, we look for Texas Long horns. We should have twenty-five head, somewhere between here and two miles down the road. The boys say we only need a dozen today. They have already been sold to the rancher next door. The son of the cowboy is here with two cow dogs from their ranch. We're going to push the cows a few miles. We see the Long horns and we go after them. The dogs are experts. What a wonderful job they are doing! We sit on our horses and watch the dogs turn the small herd toward the new owner's ranch. He is glad to see us pushing Long horns through his gate. He says howdy to us, and tells us to step down from our horses and have a soda pop. The rancher has a big corral full of wild Texas mustangs. They are for sale or trade. He has too many horses, and he needs to thin out the herd. He makes a deal with the cowboys. The rancher would like the rest of the Long horns as an even trade for fifteen wild mustangs. The cowboys are very happy. They have lots of work ahead, breaking these horses to sell.

And I am going to help. What a great day in the life of a baby cowboy! We all take a look at the horses. They all look nice, except for two or three of them. But the cowboys take the entire corral. This is great! We have lots of strong corrals for the horses, but no barn. I've never in my life seen this many wild Texas mustangs. They are like no other pony I've ever met. They don't know much of mankind. They are very easy to excite. The cowboys are going to move the horses very soon. First, we have to round up the rest of the Texas Long horn cattle. We will do that tomorrow. We say goodbye to the rancher, then ride back and unsaddle. I wash the horses down, and brush them all around. I throw them some flakes of very nice hay, and they are happy. When I get home, I give my aunts a cowboy update. They are so very thrilled of my adventure in the Lone Star State, but they need me to shop tomorrow; my uncle will be gone a few more days. After I get cleaned up and have supper, I play my guitar until I fall asleep.

The next morning I wake up early. After I dress, I sit out front. I am thinking that, in a few hours or so, the little old lady cowgirls will be up and moving around. I hope that they are doing fine. I'll be back to help them in no time. I miss them. My aunts are up and cooking. After we eat, we call a cab to take us to work. My aunts never drive a car. They walk a lot, but not at five o'clock in the morning. The cowboys call the shop looking for me. My aunt tells her son that she needs me today. I can be the baby cowboy tomorrow. I clean the place. I do the windows, sweep and take out the trash. I'm happy to help my aunts. They need a few pick-ups and drop-offs. On my way back to the shop, I stop at the burger house and get lunch for my aunts and me. My little cousins are in summer camp. Maybe I'll get a chance to see them before I leave Texas. After we have lunch, I sit out front and fall asleep in the chair in the shade. It is a very hot Texas day with very little wind to speak of. After awhile, I go inside and my aunt needs me to run a few errands down the street. There is lots of action up and down the town. I am glad to be back in Texas. Up ahead, I see some kids that I met the last time I was here. We are happy to see each other. They still live behind the dry cleaning shop. We say that we'll get together one day soon. I make it back to the shop. I have a few items from the store, and one pick-up. My aunts call a cab and the day is over.

Most of the night, I toss and turn. I can't sleep. I'm thinking of wild Texas mustangs. I'm sure the cowboys have moved some of the horses and all of the Long horns.

The next morning, the cowboys pick me up about six o'clock. At the ranch, they have separated the boy horses from the girl horses. What a fabulous sight to see. They are wild! No one has ever been on their backs, and they know nothing of mankind. They jump at everything. I'm sure they have seen birds before, but now they act as though this is their first time. When a bird flies and sits on the top rail of the corral, or the wind blows, or a leaf falls from a tree- the horses get spooked. I think these Texas wranglers can handle this wild bunch of mustangs. We run to catch and saddle four horses that are not wild. I stay aboard my pony. I have a front row seat to all the action. The cowboys have ropes. They each ride inside a pen. They catch a pony, and lead him out into a big empty round pen. They each pony their horses around in circles for an hour or so. We take a soda pop break. The cowboys are going to work three horses at a time. They say they are not going to rush these mustangs. A little while later, we bed down all the horses with fresh water and fresh hay. On our way home, we stop at the ranch of the cowboy and his son, to look at some of their new mustang horses. They have six horses that are broke and trained very well. They say I can ride whenever I get the time.

I'm home now, and my uncle is back from his trip. My two aunts are home also. We cowboy update until late at night. They are thrilled that I have the chance to see a herd of wild Texas mustang horses. The next morning, I go to work with my uncle. When we get inside, my mother is on the phone. We talk for awhile, and she tells me to be a good boy and to pay attention. I help around the shop, until the cowboys come for me after lunch. The boys are digging a new water well today, so they go out in the pasture and catch the blind mustang pony for me to ride. As I ride, I notice that he is not as calm as before. He is looking around. He can't see, but he can hear a rattle snake. He stops and side passes; he's dancing. I turn him in a tight circle. Now I can hear noise I have never heard before. I see two big Texas rattle snakes moving off into the deep grass. This is the first time I have ever seen a snake. I got a real good look at them. I think they are wonderful creatures! My pony has calmed down, and I ride down to check on the cowboys. They say that lots of snakes live here. "Keep your eyes open, John Wayne." My pony is blind, but he warned me of the snakes. We take a soda pop break and then the cowboys catch another pony for me to ride. She is a Saddlebred black and white paint, and she has a one-year-old colt that is a fabulous black beauty. This paint is a big pony- tall like a race horse. I ride around, with the colt following us for a few hours. We ride over in the next pasture with the cattle. I see three new baby cows getting milk from their mothers. I get back to the cowboys, and the day is over. When I get home, I eat, take a bath and go to sleep early. I miss my mama and I want to go home. I don't think I will go any time soon, though. There are still more horses for me to ride. And, I don't have to trespass on someone's land to ride a pony.

The next morning at the shop, I have lots of chores to do, and errands to run. It's another wonderful hot Texas morning, and I'm walking down the street, thinking of the little old ladies back home in Arkansas. I hope they are doing well. After I finish my errands, the cowboys pick me up to go to the ranch. Once we're there, they tell me to catch a pony to ride, and to be sure and watch out for snakes. There are lots to choose from today. The horses are very near. I rope the blind pony and ride for an hour or so. I see a dark horse that I want to ride. I walk down to ask the boys about the pony. They tell me to ride any pony I want. I get a soda pop and walk back out in the pasture. I saddle the dark pony, and ride down to see the boys work the mustangs. The son is here and looks like he's going to ride a wild horse. The kid gets his saddle from the truck, and jumps into the small, round pen with the mustang that he caught a few days ago. The pony runs around the pen. I don't think he likes the looks of things. The kid ropes the pony, and ties him to the fence post. He gets a soda pop and walks around looking the pony over. He starts to brush the pony, and soon, the blanket and saddle are on the mustang's back. The pony jumps a little, but he's fine. The bit is next. Cold steel is what he feels. He's licking and sucking. He likes the bit. The cowboy lets the pony run around the pen in circles. After half an hour, the kid jumps the pony. Before he could get set in the saddle, the mustang did what mustangs do. He went wild, bucking and kicking. The pony stood up in the air, but the cowboy stayed on! The pony ran faster and faster around the pen, bucking more, and kicking higher. All of a sudden, he just stopped. The kid flew right over the horse's head, over the corral fence, and into the water tub! The wrangler is fine. The pony is just standing still in the middle of the pen. The cowboy walks it off, and then jumps the pony again. This time he tells me to open the gate. He runs, bucking and kicking his way to freedom. Out in the pasture he's calming down. He sees the rest of the herd. The kid has the pony making small circles, and the mustang is now walking slow and easy. The kid gets about 50 yards from the herd and turns the pony around heading back to the corrals. The kid dismounts, and lets the mustang walk around half-an-hour or so before giving him a bath. This is the pony's first bath, besides rain water. He likes the water hose. He's trying to drink from the hose. The cowboys call it a day, and we're on our way back to town. This is the first time I have seen a cowboy break and train a pony. What an adventure in the life of a baby cowboy!

The next morning when I wake up, there is a note from my aunt on my bed. It tells me to stay home today. So I fall back to sleep dreaming of a pony. When I wake up, it's noon. I have never in my life stayed in bed so long. I play my guitar. I'm going to have a new song for my little old lady cowgirls. So, I must play every day until I get it right. The phone rings and it's my aunt calling from the shop. She wants me to stay home because my little girl cousin, Peach, is coming home today from summer camp. No one is sure what time she will be home. I sit out front and play a little while before going back inside to eat. I lay on the sofa and fall back to sleep. Later, everyone comes home. My cousin has gotten taller. We are happy to see each other. It's been awhile. She and I talk until late.

The next morning, I go to work with my uncle. We are going to be busy today. The girls are going to town to shop. When they get back, I'll be going to the ranch. I get started with my chores. The morning rushes by very fast. My uncle makes me sit out front from time to time. It is such a hot place to work- even with all of the big blow fans. It's something a person has to get used to. The girls are back, and they have lots of bags. The cowboys are here to get me. They plan to break a pony a day, and hope the doctor stays away.

At the ranch, the two cowboys and the kid each saddle a wild horse. I'm walking out in the pasture, and looking to catch the Saddlebred pony with the black colt. I see the two of them standing alone, down in the trees. I catch the mother and lead her back to the holding pens. I put my Texas saddle on her. We ride out, with the colt following us. When we find the rest of the herd, the colt stays and plays, while his mother and I ride through the gate into the next pasture. There are more horses and cows here. I see a big red pony. I must ride him. I tie off the Saddlebred paint horse, and I catch Big Red. He has no shoes, but his hooves look good. I asked the wranglers about these horses a few days ago, and they said I could ride any pony on the ranch. So, I unsaddle the paint pony and throw the saddle on Big Red. What a thrill! He is such a wonderful looking pony. I only hope he's as good as he looks. As I step up on Big Red, he moves out fast. "Easy, big boy," I say to him as I pull back gently. I make him spin a few large, then small circles. What a fine riding pony he is! He and I ride an hour or so, before I see another pony that I like. I have never seen a pony this color. He has many black and white spots- like a fire dog at the fire station. His tail is long and black, and his mane is black and white. What a beauty! I ride close to the pony, but he walks away. I dismount Big Red and tie him off. I start walking in big circles around the spot pony, and he stops. He does not like my rope, so I drop it on the ground. My circles get smaller, until I reach out, and touch his face. I stick my fingers in the side of his mouth. He licks my hand, and I rub him all over, as I remove my belt and put it around his neck. I lead him to the rope. My pants are falling and I rope the pony and put my belt back on. After I saddle him, I ride through the gate, back into the pasture, and down to the holding pens and corrals, where the wranglers are breaking mustangs today. I want to find out what kind of pony you call this spot horse.

The cowboys are riding their horses around in the round pens. I missed all the wild action. The kid is going to take his pony down the road. The two cowboys are gong to ride in the pasture with other horses and cattle. This is the first time theses horses have been around trained livestock. The cowboys are making cow ponies out of these mustangs. They have sold almost all of the herd. Soon, these horses will be working on a Texas ranch. I unsaddle my pony and take a soda pop break. When the boys return, we call it a day. And they say, "Give that Appaloosa pony a little hay, John Wayne Jay."

When I get home, my aunt says that tomorrow night we will be heading back to Arkansas. I play my guitar and sing a song, as we all get ready for bed. My cousin, Peach, and I stay up a little while longer playing checkers. She has beaten me five times in a row. *This is a great time to say goodnight.* I sleep late the next day. My aunt is packing and my uncle and his wife are working at the shop. Peach and I are going shopping today. She wants to take me on a tour. The cowboys found out about my leaving tonight, and they stop over to say goodbye. They have a new black cowboy hat for me. This is my very first cowboy hat! I thanked them for all they had done for me. They drop Peach and me off downtown. After shopping, we walk over to the dry cleaners and help my aunts and uncle for a few hours. After we get home, I eat and get ready for our trip. My uncle drives us to the train station. We say goodbye, until next summer. There are lots of people here tonight. "Look!" my uncle yells. "There's my grandson and his mother coming back from a trip up north!" It's my baby cowboy cousin. We're glad to see each other. He and his mother are coming to Arkansas next year. We say goodbye and off we go. *Thank you, Lord, for another fabulous adventure in the life of a baby cowboy.*

The next day I sleep most of the afternoon. I'm thrilled to be home. No one knows that I'm back yet. I walk around the circle. I pass the houses where the sweet little old lady cowgirls once lived. Somehow, I still feel their presence. I go and see my new cowgirls to let them know that I am back. We are so glad to see each other. They say that they have lots of work for me to help them with. I tell them I will spend the day with them tomorrow. I rush home and pick up the gifts I have for my sisters and brother. My mama is so happy to see me. I am one of her gifts in life. The kids aren't home yet from swimming. Cleopatra and I update for hours. When the kids return, we talk and play until I fall asleep.

The next morning, I ride my bike down the hill, through the woods behind my house. I'm going to see my classmate, the baby cowboy with all the dogs. He's not home, but his mother is glad to see me. She will let him know that I'm back in town as soon as he arrives home. He's out hunting with his father now and should be home tomorrow. I want to go see the horses down behind the gas station, but I think I'll wait for the baby cowboy. When I get back home, my aunt and I cowboy update until supper is ready.

The carnival is in town and my mother is on the phone telling my aunt that she will take me and the kids. I go next door to the big kid's house. He's home for a change. He tells me that I could work with him at the carnival, and gives me five free tickets. I ask him if they have any horses there, and he says they only have a merry-go-round with fake horses. I thanked him for the tickets, but I don't think I want to work there. I can see real horses at the country fruit stand. When I get home, my aunt is on the phone with Rex and Billy Bob. They are in New York City for most of the summer. Rex said his daddy will pick me up one day soon, and that he and I will take a ride. He doesn't like for me to trespass, and ride other people's horses without permission from the owners. After talking with the boys, I go home to my mother. She tells me to stay home tomorrow. The next morning, I'm up early. I'm sitting on the back steps thinking of Texas, and the legendary adventures I had there. I thought of the people I met, my Texas saddle and very nice black hat, the pride of the Lone Star State-Texas Long horn cattle, and wild mustangs. I also thought about that blind pony.

CHAPTER NINE

My mother is going to take me to meet a blind man tomorrow. She works across the street from him and his newspaper stand. He's going to love hearing about how I rode the blind mustang pony and how we walked within eye sight of a couple of rattle snakes. My mama comes out and sits with me before she goes to work. She's going to take all of us kids out tonight.

After a short time, my mama is back from work. We are going to the carnival. Once we all get cleaned up, we go to my aunt's house. She calls a cab, and off we go. There are lots of people everywhere. We play games, and take lots of rides on the midway grounds. I have fun just watching all the people and all the action. My aunt is also having a great time. I see lots of kids from school and we talk a short time. The big wheel in the sky is stuck, with many people aboard, yelling and screaming for help. And that was going to be my next ride- but, not now! They have the fire department and midway workers helping all the people get off of the ride safely. Everyone is fine. My mama wants to makes sure we stay on the ground. So, we ride the bumper cars next. We are having a great time, and mama says we will come back one more time before the carnival leaves town. Then, we catch a cab, drop my aunt off, and we go home to sleep.

The next morning, I catch the baby cowboy feeding his dogs at five o'clock. We are going to meet at the gas station in two hours. He says the horses are there. I rush back home and everyone is still sleeping. I get my guitar and sit out front and play by my mother's bedroom window. She looks out with happy eyes and tells me that I'm her alarm clock. She over sleeps just a little. When Cleopatra is ready, I walk her half way to her work place. She kisses me, and tells me to be careful and stay alert, and to pay attention. It's unspoken, but she knows by the look in my eye, that I'm on a baby cowboy mission. She wants me to be at her job at four o'clock. Today is the day I will meet the blind man. The kids are up when I return home. I tell my big sister of my plans, and she is not too happy. She never wants me to trespass, and she's always afraid for me. My sister loves me and doesn't want to see me hurt, in trouble, or killed over a pony. I get my gear and off I go. The baby cowboy is early and he's thrilled to be pony scouting today. The horses are in another pasture far from where they once lived. We ride fast on our bikes through the woods and suddenly, we see the horses. I've never been this far, but the cowboy knows this country very well. He has been here many times hunting with his father. We drop the bikes in the bush. I climb a tree and I can see for miles. Most of what I see are tree tops. We're smack dab in the middle of the forest. The baby cowboy and I swap places. I cross over the stream and rope a pony. I ride him to my pal and then he has lots of fun riding on the pony. The only time he rides is when he is with me. He is still a little afraid of horses- but he's getting better.

When I get home, my sister is glad to see me. I play with the kids awhile before I go downtown to meet my mother at her job at the Dinner House. It's the same place where Billy Bob and Rex had a party for me last year. I see my mama crossing the street. We walk half a block to the newsstand. The little old grey headed white man with dark glasses and a long stick yells, "Is that you, Cleopatra?" "Yes, sir," she says to the man. He hugs and kisses my mother. At the same time, cars are pulling up to the stand for newspapers. The blind man is also counting money, selling candy, and shining shoes. My mother leaves me with the man for an hour while she shops and pays bills down the street. "Howdy, John Wayne, I heard about your jump from the second-floor. Couldn't you have just used the door, kid?" He tells me that my mother worked for his mother until she passed away to heaven. The man said, "I knew your mother when she was a teenager, in town from Texas, to stay with her aunt. That's when she started working for my mother. So, do you understand, kid?" "Yes, sir. I do." I'm at the age where I'm asking lots of questions- but only to myself at this point. I'll ask my mother later. "Take a seat, kid." He cleans and shines my boots. At the same time, he is selling papers. His place is a small store. He always gives the right change. I'm paying close attention. *How does he do that so well?* "I know what you're thinking, kid. I've been blind all of my life." Cleopatra is back and the man says, "Your mama is returning. I know her fragrance. Come back and see me, John Wayne." "Thank you for the shine and the time, sir," I answer. My mother hugs and kisses him and off we go. As we walk back home, my mom tells me to always pay close attention to the blind man. "I've known him most of my life and he's a wonderful man. Your boots look very nice. When he shines your boots, it's a sign that he likes you. I worked for his family for many years. He is going to need you one day, baby cowboy. You just be ready. I told him about the blind pony you rode in Texas. He doesn't smile much, but he really got a kick when hearing of that adventure."

We are back home, and the kids are not here. I get my bike and ride around. I see them down the hill behind the school playing with kids from my class. I yell for them to come home. When they get inside, my mother has new shoes for all of us.

The next day, I do my chores then I rush to my aunt's house to help her. I check the ladies out. Some are still sleeping. The landlord says at noon, I could sell fruit out in the country. That is great news! When I finish helping the ladies, I tell my aunt I am going to go pony scouting while selling fruits and vegetables. She tells me to be careful.

After setting up the stand, the boss leaves. He will be back at six o'clock. I want to go down the hill scouting, but not just yet. I have my first customer of the day pulling in. The two ladies are happy to see me. They know me from a few years ago. They buy lots of items and I thank them. I put the bags in the car for the ladies. Two more cars are pulling in. People get out to shop. They are lost. I give them directions to where they want to go. More and more people are coming. It's almost nonstop action- like on the backside of the racetrack! I start to wonder if I will get to see a horse today. As I look around, there's not much left to sell. Suddenly, a man and woman come in and buy everything I have left. *This is great!* I rush down the hill, through the woods and over the fence. I see tracks and I get excited. I have always thought about these ponies that are out too far for me to reach on my bike. I have missed them. And I've sold all of the apples and carrots. I'm sorry I did that. I see the herd and they hear me, but they don't see me yet. I climb the tree near me, for a better view. I can see all around me. No one is here except the horses and I. There are more than before, and they all have shoes. I'm happy to know that someone is riding them. My string rope is ready. I climb down, and walk slow and easy to the herd. I catch a bay mare. I grab a handful of mane and jump on her. I walk her close to the fruit stand. What a nice pony! I tie her off and I rush back to the stand. I don't know what time it is, but it should be almost time for me to ride a little while longer, just down the hill where I can hear the boss coming. His truck makes a lot of noise. *Thank you, Lord.* Another legendary day through the eyes of a baby cowboy. I ride another half-hour. Then I rub the pony and turn her loose. She is happy to get back to the herd. When I get back to the stand, I hear the boss coming up the road. He has happy eyes. There is nothing to pick up- just me and the money. He's a happy man. He knows that I did a good job when I worked for his mother and father, but he didn't expect me to sell out of everything. We get home, and I sit out front and talk with my aunt. She tells me of the many reasons that she loves me. She is most happy that I am a fabulous shepherd for the Lord's flock of ponies around the nation. She tells me I'm a baby cowboy sensation, and a wonderful peacemaker. She thanked me for being so very helpful to her girlfriends- the sweet little old black lady cowgirls from days long ago. Her eyes are getting red, and I think she is going to cry. She feels really bad that she has lived here all these years and never talked much to my new, sweet little old white lady cowgirls. She's happy now that they all speak to one another. She tells me that the three ladies I helped from the rooming house fire are going to Bible study with her this Sunday.

The next morning I ride my bike downtown, past my mother's work place. I pass the blind man's newsstand. I'm headed way uptown, just riding around. It's almost daylight, and the wonderful little town is waking up. People are going to their jobs. I've made the big circle from downtown, to uptown. Now I am on a mission. I want to smell a pony! I want to touch a pony! I'm at the train station, and I jump my bike down across the tracks, and off I go. I pass the Hobo Trail and the country store. The store's not open yet. When I get close to the pasture, I can smell horses. I'm going left, off the tracks. I hide my bike, and over the wire I go. I hear horses, and I keep walking. I see hoof prints in the dirt. I see fresh horse manure. And there, just ahead of me, stand four of God's most fabulous creatures, looking me right in the face. I know these ponies, and they know me. I reach out and touch all four horses. I rub them awhile, and they just stand still. I have no apples or carrots, but I don't think they mind at all. They have lots of green grass and fresh water, and they feel the love I have for each of them. I climb a tree to see if the coast is clear. No one is here. I climb back down to the bottom of the tree trunk, and sit and watch. What a nice string of horses they are. I say goodbye, until we meet again. I ride up to the other pasture. I hide my bike, and under the wire fence I go, deep into the woods. I find a few head of horses. There are many more out in the pasture, but it's too far to walk. These ponies are new. I don't recall seeing them on my last trip out here. I string rope the black one. I rub him down, and lead him around. The other horses run toward the herd in the middle of the pasture. I tie the pony off to a tree and pick up his feet. He has a big nail stuck in his hoof. I can't pull it out. I check his other feet. There is a rock in his back left foot. I find a strong stick and pick out the rock. Now, I think about what I'm going to do about that big nail. I recall seeing a strip of wire over by my bike. I rush to get it. The wire is about six feet long. I wrap wire around the head of the big nail and tie the other end off to the tree. I take my string rope from his neck. When he walks, he pulls the nail right out of his hoof. He runs to the herd, with his tail flying high in the air, as if to say, "Thank you, baby cowboy!"

I stop at the country store for a soda pop. When I get to my aunt's house, she is out front having tea with her new friends- the three ladies from the rooming house. While they talk, I go inside and play my guitar until I fall asleep. I'm up in time to help my aunt around the house and check on the little old ladies before I go to the country fruit stand. Everything is loaded and ready to go. My boss says that I don't have to come out to work every day. He says he knows that school is getting ready to start, and that I should play a little bit more. I think to myself, *If he only knew!*

After we set up the stand, the boss says bye and off he goes. I didn't ride a pony the day before, so after a few sales, I run down the hill scouting for any sign of horses. I don't smell, see, or hear a pony. There are no tracks. I climb a tree, and I see people at the fruit stand. Then, I turn around and see the herd. They are a long way off. I've got to get back to the stand. I come down the tree easy, and suddenly I hear the sounds of hooves pounding the ground! There are more ponies coming fast, like race horses, in the woods. They stop right underneath the tree. Slowly, I ease down the tree. I should hit the ground, but I want action! So, I do what the little old lady cowgirls once said I should do. I drop out of the tree onto the back of one of the horses, without any fear. The pony takes off, moving fast through the woods, out into wide open pasture. I have two hands full of mane and I'm holding on for dear life. This could be my greatest ride ever! I must get control, or it may be my last ride ever. He's not wild, he's just happy and feeling good. Suddenly, we get near the herd, and he stops. I remove the string rope from my back pocket and lean forward to slip the rope around his face; a baby cowboy headset. It works great. Now I have control of his head. I'm looking around, and I've never been this deep in my trespassing adventures. I'm out a few miles from the fruit stand, with the entire herd of horses following me and my newfound friend. He's a wonderful grey and black pony. As I ride, I get the funny feeling that I will be getting fired today. I'm too far to turn around now. I ride to the end of the pasture. It must be five miles from fence to fence. I see no houses or roads, until I go down the trail a bit more. Now I see the country dirt road and cars. I also see the main gate. I turn back toward the fruit stand. When I get close, I take off one of my tee shirts and wipe the pony down very well. He just stands there watching me, as I walk from the woods, under the fence, then out of sight. As I go up the hill behind the stand, I look back and the pony is standing at the fence, still watching me.

When I get to the stand, there is not a fruit or vegetable in sight. I am thinking that this baby cowboy just got jacked! Nothing is left except empty boxes. I see the boss man coming. He has a big smile on his face. He thinks I sold out. Instead, I was robbed. He laughs and say's, "Don't worry, John Wayne, I have insurance." As I pick up loose crates and boxes, I see a red can nailed to the post. I stand on a box and get the can. There is a note, and all of the money is here for the fruits and vegetables. The note is from the two little ladies that know me from some years ago. They took everything and left over two hundred dollars, plus the twenty dollars I sold before I went pony scouting. The boss is still happy but tells me to stay close to the stand at all times. What a day in the life of a baby cowboy.

When I get home, my aunt tells me that the baby cowboys' fathers will be picking me up at ten o'clock tomorrow morning to ride horses. Rex and Billy Bob are still out of town. When they arrive the next morning, they tell me I can bring a friend. I call my baby cowboy classmate and he says he can go with us. I'm thinking that this will be good for him. When we arrive at the ranch, the mothers are glad to see my friend and me. We eat, and then head out to the barn. Three horses are all ready to go. I saddle a pony for the baby cowboy. This should be great for his confidence. He has never been in a saddle. I help him on his pony, and we all ride out to the pasture, and then over through the next two pastures. I've been here with Rex and Billy Bob. This is the new pasture for the race horses that will be coming here in a few months. The baby cowboy is having a fine time. And he is looking like a real pro.

They have lots of cattle this year. The father says the boys will be back tomorrow night, and that we will all have a swim very soon. "You bring the baby cowboy with you, John Wayne." We ride over to scout a few head of cattle. The father is happy to have us out at the ranch. He tells us we are always welcome. As we start back, we go off the main trail to let the baby cowboy feel the thrill of riding across the stream. He loved it. We scout a while before crossing back over the water and back to the barn. Once we unsaddle the horses, my pal and I hose the horses down and groom them all over. The boys' fathers are drinking a beer. They tell us to come inside when we finish. The stalls are clean and the horses all have fresh, clean water. I throw them a few flakes of very good hay and I make sure the stalls are locked. We go inside to get cleaned up. The ladies have supper ready for us. School starts next week, and the parents are going to have a party for the boys. They invite me and the baby cowboy. It's a pool party and there will be lot of kids. After we finish eating, the fathers will take us back. The mothers hug and kiss our little black faces and tell us they love us. We thank the ladies, and off we go. We drop off my pal, and then I get dropped off at my aunt's house. The little old lady cowgirls see me, and call for me to come over. They need me to go shopping when I get a chance.

My aunt is glad to see me. She is baking cakes, and she needs a few items from the store. After I take a bath and get dressed, I round up the shopping lists and money from the ladies, and off I go to the store. I rush back with my aunt's items first, so she can finish baking. It takes about half-an-hour to shop for my friends. They are so happy that I have time to help them all. The girls want to talk to me about when they were young. They tell me that they were cowgirls working with their fathers on farms and ranches all across the country. It was a very exciting time for them. Ten of these little ladies owned their own horses, and were cowgirls in the state fairs all around the country for many years. The guitar lady comes down and plays a song. They tell me that if I have time that they can teach me a song. I run across the street to get my guitar. We play and sing, long past the cowgirls bedtime, and they don't mind. My aunt tells me to go home to my mama. She hugs and kisses me, and off I go on my bike. The kids are eating supper, and my mother is working late tonight. After being home awhile, I ride my bike downtown to my mother's job. I look through the window, and see that Cleopatra is almost finished. When she comes out, she rides the bike, while I sit on the handle bars. We are home in no time. The next day, my classmate is still thrilled about the pony ride at the ranch. And we didn't have to trespass. He tells me to stay away from the horses down behind the gas station, because sooner or later we're going to get into big trouble. He is not going to trespass anymore. I understand what he is saying, but I really don't care. The baby cowboy is a dog boy. He likes horses, but he loves dogs- lots of dogs. I love all of God's creatures, but I really, really love horses- lots and lots of horses. A *No Trespassing* sign and some wire will not keep me away from a pony. And I don't care who owns that pony. If I think the pony needs a baby cowboy's touch, I will touch him. I ask my pal if he would like to go to the pool party next week. He says he'll ask his mother and let me know.

I am going to go talk to the blind man. When I get to the newspaper stand, my new pal is giving shoe shines and selling papers and books. He senses that I'm near him. "Howdy, John Wayne. How are you, kid?" "Fine, sir. How are you?" "I'm glad you stopped by. I need you to sit and pay attention." "Yes, sir." So, I stay with Mr. blind man all day until his helper arrives late. I must say, this man is fabulous. How does he do all of these things without any eye sight? I can see, and I couldn't clean and shine a shoe that well. "Kid, I need you to help me this winter when the race horses come to town. You're going to sell racing forms and tip sheets. Kid, I think this will be good for you to work a few hours after school." "That sounds great, sir." "Kid, you can go home now. Say hello to your mother." Then he gives me ten dollars and a candy bar. "Thank you, sir." And off I go, on my bike, back home to my mom.

No one is home, so I ride to my aunt's and everyone is there having supper. My daddy called today and talked with my aunt. Rex and Billy Bob also called to make sure I remember about the party. We say goodnight to my aunt and we go home. I play my guitar until I fall asleep. My mother always comes and removes the guitar from my bed. I sleep late the next morning. After the kids eat, I take them uptown window shopping. My sisters really love to window shop. We see lots of kids we know from school. So, we spend time talking in the park on Bath House Row. What a wonderful town we live in. It's getting hot, so I buy the kids some ice cream. Walking back from town, we stop at my brother's daddy's house for a visit. I leave my brother there. Cleopatra will pick him up when she gets off work tonight. My sisters and I walk down to the music store. We go inside and I buy strings for one of my guitars. We walk past the train station, across the tracks and over the bridge, through the Hobo Trail to our aunt's house. She is glad to see us and thinks that we should go across the street and sing for the ladies. I restring my guitar and my sisters and I go to play and sing songs. The girls are thrilled to have us over. They make snacks for us. I guess it's a party! They teach us a song. So, I play and we all sing along together. It's great- just like old times in the circle again. As we say goodbye, the girls say that they need me tomorrow.

Our aunt has supper ready, so we eat and go home. We play with the kids next door, until my mother and the baby come home. After everyone is asleep, my mother and I sit out on the back steps and talk. She tells me the blind man is troubled about my trespassing adventures. He's worried I might get hurt or something worse. "Let's face it, cowboy, you're breaking the law. Cellulose John Wayne Jay, you are not to trespass on anyone's land again. Do you understand? What if you get hurt far from home, all alone? Who is going to help you; a pony? No. You're going to help yourself by staying off those white folks' land. Leave their ponies alone." I begin to cry, and only I, really know why. Cleopatra looks at me and says, "Shut up, before I give you something to cry about." And she goes inside and falls asleep on the sofa. I sit out back, thinking about all the horses that I may never touch again. No more pony scouting. I don't know if I can do this, but I'm going to try. I can always ride with my friends, Rex and Billy Bob. And the race horses will be back soon. My mother always tells me there is more to life than a pony. I go in and wake my mama. She'll feel better in her own bed. She hugs and kisses me and tells me how much she loves me.

The next morning I'm working for my aunt, helping her do chores around her three houses. When I finish, I check on the lady cowgirls. While they are getting shopping money and a list together, the big boss man arrives. I tell him I can't work the fruit stand anymore this summer. He thanked me and he thanked me again for helping his mama and daddy. The girls are ready. Some need me to go to the wash house and some need me to go to the store. So, I'll get the wash started first, and then I'll go shopping. The man with only one arm who is the owner of the wash house has known me for years. He and his wife are very thrilled that I am a wonderful peacemaker. They know that I'm helping the ladies. So, he tells me to go shop for the girls and he would wash and dry, so that when I finish shopping, I can come back and everything will be ready to go. I thank him and off I go down to the store. Reverend Jones with the Great Dane is here, without the dog. He's saving souls today and everyday. I tell him that my sisters and my brother and I will be in church this Sunday morning in time for Bible study. He is overjoyed and he has tears in his eyes. He has known me since I was a baby cowboy and this will be my first time to his church. The Reverend Jones let me ride my first creature ever;

his big Great Dane. When I finish shopping, I rush back to the cowgirls. I drop off the food and I go for the ladies' wash. Everything is nice and neat, and ready and waiting for me. The girls are getting a treat. Some of the cowgirls and I sit and drink soda pop. Suddenly, a lady comes down the stairs with a picture of herself and four girls. They all live here today. The picture is of the cowgirls, many years ago. As I see the picture and look around me, I see five beautiful faces sitting right here with me. We cowboy update for hours, as more girls bring out pictures of themselves with their wonderful horses. "When you, John Wayne, were the stick horse baby cowboy, we wanted to share these pictures with you. But times didn't permit. Today times are changing for the better. We love you, baby cowboy. There was no real peace around here until you moved into the circle. Some of us have been here for forty years, and we have seen you bridge a lot of gaps. And we thank you from the bottom of our hearts." "Cowgirls, you're going to make me cry. Bye-bye."

As I walk down the stairs to the sidewalk, I look back at the girls sitting on the big front porch. They all have happy eyes but they say to me, "Please, John Wayne, our only baby cowboy, we need you to stop trespassing, sonny boy." I run back to my aunt's house thrilled and overjoyed. These ladies act as if they are my mamas. I think they really, truly, love me. So, I feel good that I had the chance to meet all the horses close to my house, but I've got to give it up. I don't hear voices, but I do know that the sweet little old black lady cowgirls would tell me not to press my luck. I'm very blessed not to have been hurt or killed already.

CHAPTER TEN

I cowboy update with my aunt because for the last two hours I've been cowgirl updating. I say to my aunt that I'm done pony scouting and trespassing on other people's land, and fooling around with their livestock without permission from anyone but myself. School starts next week and if I don't stop trespassing, I won't make it to the second grade at Goldstein- my schoolhouse. With tears in her eyes, my aunt hugs and kisses me and tells me it will be hard to stop this thing called "horse-fever." "You've been sick with horse-fever for a long time, and you've got it real bad." She smiles, then laughs out loud and tells me to go home to my mama.

The next morning, Cleopatra, the kids, and I go to church. At about the same time, across in the circle, history is being made. I feel my cowgirls from heaven smiling down on all of us in the circle. My aunt is going back to her white church of a dozen years or more, in tow with her newfound girlfriends- the three little ladies I helped out of the burning house. As you recall, my aunt and I could not attend Bible study there a few years ago. My aunt has been back once, with her black friend. This morning, she's back with three wonderful little old white ladies. They have lived next door to one another for over twenty years with much hate between them. But today, I can truly say that peace is in the town, with love all around. My classmate, the baby cowboy, is in Sunday school. He says he will go to the party tomorrow. I tell him to be home and ready by noon. When church is over, I go home and change, and off to my aunt's house I go. I want to know what happened at her church. She's not home yet, so I go in and call my pal, Rex. They will pick me up at one o'clock tomorrow. He and Billy Bob are so excited. It's been awhile since we have all been together. The boys have been fishing and have caught lots of fish for the party. They also tell me about the four horses they are going to bring for all the kids to ride.

My aunt is home now, and she has three girls from next door, and two more ladies from church with her. They are going to have a tea party. I say hello, and I go around the circle to play with the kids. After awhile, I ride my bike downtown. When I get to the newspaper stand, my blind friend is having lunch. He's so happy to smell and feel my presence. "Kid, I don't want you hurt or killed. Will you stop trespassing?" "Yes, sir. I have already stopped." "Good, John Wayne. Cleopatra told me about how you rode the blind pony. Well, this blind man needs you today. Can you stay?" "Yes, sir. I can." He gives me pocket change and small dollar bills to make change. I'm selling products from the stand. People pull right up to the sidewalk and get whatever they need. I stay until six o'clock. The helper is here now. My blind friend gives me ten dollars and thanks me for helping. "Come and see me when you can, my little man. Say hello to your mother for me." I say goodbye and off I go to my mama. Glad I could help him. Ten dollars is a lot of money for a kid my age during these times. But I do what I do for reasons other than money. And I really can't explain it.

I rush home on my bike. I give my mama ten dollars. She's thrilled. She makes fifteen dollars a week on one job and twenty a week on her other job. I made ten bucks in a few hours. I'm just not thrilled about a dollar. I'd rather have a pony in my front yard. After supper the kids go to sleep. The moon is so bright tonight. I talk to my mother until she falls asleep. I go sit out on the back steps in the moonlight. I'm thinking about those ponies down behind the gas station, and those down by the train tracks. I can't forget that fabulous herd behind the country fruit stand; the horses I had to break the law in order just to touch. It's true that I did a lot more than touch a few. I could be considered a baby horse-thief in most circles. I'm not sleep walking, but I do walk down the back steps and get on my bike. The moon is just so bright. I'm very sick. I have what's called pony-fever. I ride fast down the hill behind my house, through the woods onto the street, past the corner store and gas station. I ride past where the horses live. I see a truck parked on the side of the road, with a man behind the truck doing some work. He has a picture of a horse on the door of his truck. I say hello to the white man, and ask, "Are you in trouble?" He is kind of in a little baby state of shock. He takes a second look, and asks, "What is this little black boy doing way out here on the highway this late at night?" "I can't sleep, so I'm riding my bike." "I'm out of gas, kid. I need you to get me some gas. I have a gas can- if I can find it. Will you help me?" "Yes, sir. I will. Are you by chance a cowboy?" "Yes, I am, kid. Are you writing a book, or are you going to come help me find the gas can? I'm drunk and my wife will kill me if I don't get home soon. Can't you see that I need you?" "I got it. I got the can, sir. Now, all I need is money." He fumbles through his pockets- I guess like a drunk man would. He's got lots of hundred dollar bills and he gives me one. I say, "Mr., I only need three dollars. I cannot carry one hundred dollars worth of gas on my bike." "Sure sonny boy, you're right. Here, take this five." I rush to the station. I get the gas and hurry back fast. The cowboy is sitting inside of the truck asleep. I put the gas in the tank, and I leave a little bit for under the hood. I wake up the cowboy. I look in the truck. He's got lots of beer cans all over the floor and seat. He raises the hood and pours a little gas inside. The truck starts right away. He gives me ten dollars and says, "Put your bike in the back, kid. I'll take you home." "No thanks, sir. You need to get home." "Do you like horses, kid?" "Yes, I do." "Here's my card with my number. Call me and you can ride my horses any time you like. My name is Leo. What's your name, kid?" "My name is Cellulose John Wayne Jay." "Well, get home before your mama has the police out here looking for you. Call me soon. Thanks again, my friend." He smiles as he drives away, down past where the horses live. I rush home and jump in bed. Everyone is still asleep. Lord, thanks for another fabulous day in the life of a baby cowboy. I lay in my bed thinking about what that white man said. *I can ride a pony anytime I want. That's not trespassing. That is owner's permission to pony scout, touch and ride any pony on his land. Oh, what a nice man! I will call him soon before he forgets.* This puts a new face on what looked like a lost cause for a pony- loving, stick horse baby cowboy. I have to get some rest. I'm falling off to sleep thinking about my little girl classmate, Princess. I miss her and I have not seen her all summer long. I wonder if she is out of town.

The next morning I do chores around the house, and I just take it easy until I am ready for the party. Princess only lives a few blocks from my house. I get my bike and ride to her house. I see her out in the front yard. She yells to me, "Howdy, baby cowboy!" We are thrilled to see one another. Her parents are not home from work. I ask her if she would like to go to a party at my friend's house. "It's a pool party at Billy Bob's house." "Will they let black kids swim?" I tell her that they will. She says she will call her daddy at his work place. Princess brings the phone to the door. Her daddy wants to talk to me. He wants information, and then he says that Princess can go. We are thrilled! I tell her to be ready around one o'clock. I rush home. My aunt is at my house. She's in the back, playing with the kids. She yells to me that Rex and Billy Bob called, and want me to bring my friends, and one of my guitars. "They will pick you up at one o'clock sharp!" *Thank you, Lord!*

My aunt is going to take the kids to the movie house because they don't want to go to the party. I tell them all goodbye as I get ready for the pool party. Before long, Rex is at the door. We're so happy to see one another. We pick up Princess and the baby cowboy. When we get to Billy Bob's house, there are lots of kids there. There are some kids there that I haven't seen since the Elvis show, on the night of my party. It's early and we are having a blast. Here comes the truck with the four horses from my pal, Rex's, ranch. I gave him his first stick horse ever and he still has it in his bedroom. I made the horse from the little old lady cowgirls' mops that I took from their back porch. I do recall the girls asking me if I knew anything about their missing brooms and mops. I rush to help the boys unload the horses. Most of the kids are in the pool. The boys' parents will put some of the kids on the horses and lead them around. My two classmates have never been around this many little white kids our own age. We meet all the kids. Some say that they have black kids at their school and they say, "Let's all take a swim." We change into our swimwear and jump in the pool. We're having lots of fun before we go back to school. The baby cowboys are having the time of their young lives! Princess has never ridden a pony, but today she is ready to ride. She asks me if I would guide her around. "Sure, I will." And we take a ride. She is having a very fine time. Kids are standing in line for a pony ride. Kids are eating, playing, talking, and the pool is still half full of kids. Billy Bob's mother wants me to play my guitar. Rex will play his drums and Billy Bob will play his piano. We boys have never played together. We've just talked about playing some day. Well, this is that day! As soon as we stop swimming and horseback riding, we go inside to practice. One of Billy Bob's classmates comes into the room with his bass guitar. This is going to be legendary! Billy Bob has been taking music classes for years. He teaches us three songs. We learn them in no time. Their mothers are dancing as we start to play. Now all the kids are dancing and having a fabulous time. I'm looking around as I play my guitar, and I ask myself, "Who *are* these guys?" My baby cowboy pals must be movie stars! I never knew two boys could have so many friends. We stop to take a short break. We've only played one song. I think it may have been the longest song in history. We played almost half-an-hour. And the kids are loving it. They want more. They are still dancing without the music and calling and yelling for more. Now I see why the boys' mothers set this music thing up like this. They just knew we were going to be sounding great! My two classmates, Princess and the baby cowboy, have lots of new friends, and as they exchange phone numbers, they will be peacemakers. Most of these kids have never played with kids of another race. Some look me in my face and say, "There's no space or place for fools hating for no reason. Could you boys please play another song?" And the rest is history. Before long, parents are picking up their kids. Most kids have to go to school tomorrow. Kids are still in the pool and some kids are still being led around by the fathers of Rex and Billy Bob. I'm looking into the happy eyes of the kids sitting on the back of these horses, and I think of my first pony ride. I was so excited. Big White was my first pony to ride. He was also the same pony Billy Bob was riding here in this yard when he got hurt. And the pony had to be put down a few years ago. Thank you, Lord, that my pal is fine. And I think I'll sing this little song of mine as the kids are leaving. They yell, "Peace, John Wayne!

See you later!" Some of the kids and parents stay and help clean up the place. I help the boys with the horses. What a fabulous day in the life of a baby cowboy! The mothers hug and kiss me, and tell me they love me, and to pay attention in school. The boys' fathers take us home and thank us for coming to the party.

When I get home, mama and the kids are there. We talk awhile before getting things ready for the big school day tomorrow. I'm just thrilled about all the new little white kids I met tonight. As I look in my pockets, I have twenty-six phone numbers. That's a lot of pals for one night! I don't have a phone, but my aunt does. The next morning I'm up early and ready for school. My baby sister is going to be in the first grade. She tells me that she had a hard time sleeping last night. Mama has a new babysitter for my baby brother right next door. After dropping the baby off, she takes us across the street to school. All the kids are happy to be in school this morning. I see my name on the list outside of the main office. I go to my new classroom. Half of the kids are here. I see Princess, but not the baby cowboy. He must be in another classroom. The teacher comes in. She calls the class to order and tells us her name. I'm thinking that if this is going to be my teacher every day, I am in love. She is wonderful! As she calls the roll, the kids must say, "Here." Now I know the baby cowboy will not be in my class this year. I miss him already. But, I'll see him at lunch or at the playground. When the bell rings for lunch, I see the baby cowboy. He loves his new class and teacher. We go and sit with Princess and her friends. She and the cowboy had a great time at the pool party last night. They thanked me for showing them how to be baby peacemakers. They didn't know how to act around all the new white kids. They were afraid the kids would not like them because they are black, but all the kids there showed us love.

After school the next day, I decide to call Mr. Leo. I get his card, and go next door to my classmate's house. She lets me call my new friend. He is happy to hear from me and tells me his kids met me at the party. He says he hasn't been able to stop thinking of the night I helped him, when he ran out of gas. He said, that for hours, no one would help him- until I appeared from the darkness with two little helping hands. "Kid, I was just too drunk to walk three miles to the gas station. And I thank you very, very much. What are you doing right now, John Wayne? I'm thinking about a pony. Do you live near the gas station?" "Yes sir, I do." Mr. Leo then told me to meet him at the station in an hour and he would show me some horses. And I could ride any pony I wanted. I ran back home after thanking my classmate for the use of the phone. I'm so happy she is in my class again this year. I love her, and she is so very smart. She plays with dolls, but also plays baseball and football with the boys. I've never seen her play basketball, but she is tall, and I'm sure she would be great at it.

I get my bike and head out to go meet the white cowboy man. I see the truck. He sees me riding fast through the station parking lot. "Howdy, John Wayne!" "Howdy, Sir!" He puts my bike in the back of the truck, and off we go down past the gas station onto the dirt road. We come to a big gate, and I see a big white house. As he gets out to open the gate, I'm thinking, *Who lives here? Jesus must live here- that's who!* I have never seen a house so big! They have two big barns, just like the barns on the backside of the racetrack. Mr. Leo takes me inside to meet his wife and kids. When we kids see each other, we just about go crazy! We start dancing, and jumping up and down and all around. They are shocked that I know their daddy. The parents are amazed at how happy the kids are to see me. "John Wayne, we had so much fun at the party!" I'm happy-eyed as I look at the kids, and recall how great they danced. They were the best out of all the kids. I got a very good look from the stage at them all having the time of their young lives. The mother and the kids go and make snacks, when the daddy tells me in my ear, "Don't tell my kids that I was drunk the night we met. Deal?" "Deal." We eat and talk. The kids also play music, but they were blown away at how great we sounded at the party. They tell me all of their friends loved our songs. Mr. Leo takes us out to the barns. As I look the place over, I'm very sure this is the ranch behind the gas station. The baby cowboy and I have been trespassing here for more than a year. I've never been to the front of the ranch until now. I've only seen the back of this wonderful piece of what all the sweet little old black, and white lady cowgirls would call, *A Slice of Heaven.*

The kids are going to saddle some horses while Mr. Leo takes me in his truck out to the pasture. We drive up on a hill and I can see the top of the gas station and the main highway. The cowboy tells me he has almost one hundred horses all around town. I ask him if he has any horses out in the country past the racetrack. "Yes I do, John Wayne." I'm very sure that the horses behind the fruit stand are Mr. Leo's. *Thank you, God in heaven. I don't have to trespass to touch a pony anymore! I have permission from the owner.* "Baby cowboy, I've got a lot of race horses and more coming soon. Would you like to work for me sometime?" "Yes, sir. I would." We head back to the barn after looking at the herd. The kids are ready, so we ride while their mother makes supper. I really want to tell the cowboy that I've trespassed on his land in two locations. I just don't want to tell him right now. We ride to four big pastures looking at the horses. I'm riding a pony that I've fed apples and carrots to before. This pony knows me well. I rode him bareback, with just a string rope around his face. I also put the baby cowboy on this pony, and walked him around for his first pony ride. My friend will be thrilled to know we don't have to trespass anymore. We will have permission. After we ride, we clean the horses very well and we eat supper. The kids want to know if my friends and I can play at their birthday party in a few months. The parents are very happy that their kids are baby peacemakers. We say goodnight, and they all take me home. My mama is sitting out on the porch when we drive up. I introduce everyone. "Miss Cleo, we love your baby cowboy, and he has been to our ranch today. We want to know if it is all right for John Wayne to ride horses at our house." "Sure he can. Thank you." And off they go.

My mama needs me to run to the wash house. That's great. I'll see all the ladies tonight. I put the wash bag on the handle bars of my bike and off I go, fast like a race horse! After I start the wash, I ride down the sidewalk. It's dark. The girls are sleeping but my aunt is sitting on the porch. She's always happy to see me. I'm her boy, ever since her kids left for college. We cowboy and cowgirl update. She is thrilled that I don't have to trespass anymore. She and the ladies are going to Bible study tomorrow night and more cowgirls are going to join them. They like being peacemakers. I go and check the wash. The clothes are ready to dry. When I get back, my aunt needs me to shop. At the store, I see the baby cowboy with his mother. He can't stop talking about the party. He is so happy about all the new kids he met. I tell him we don't have to trespass on the white folks' land ever again. I've got permission to ride the horses behind the station. His eyes lit up like bright stars! "Now, when do you want to ride?" I ask. "How about now?" "No, it's too late, and we have school tomorrow. See you." I run to give my aunt her bag of food. She kisses me and tells me I have to help her tomorrow after school. I rush back to the wash house. Everything is ready. I fold and bag the clothes, and off I go, back home.

The next day, my aunt and I clean a little at the rooming house. It's that time of year, and all the big time thoroughbreds will be here, along with some legendary Black wild horse wranglers- some are from Africa. When I finish, I grab my guitar and rush over to the cowgirls' house. They know when I'm in the circle. They always look for me from their big three-story house. Someone there is always looking out a window. We are happy to see one another. The guitar lady comes downstairs with her guitar. She tells me, "Cellulose John Wayne Jay, this is your lucky day! My guitar now belongs to you! I turn ninety-years-old today, sonny boy. Yes, it's my birthday. I also want to say that all of us girls recall when you were the stick horse baby cowboy. We loved you then, but we just didn't talk. And we love you now. It's always a party when we see you! Could you please sing us a song, sonny boy?" "Yes, I can! How about *Happy Birthday, Mary?*" Everyone sings along as I play. The birthday girl is crying. She tells me I'm a very special little black baby cowboy. And she's so blessed to know me, and she is thrilled that I was around when the house was on fire. "You saved my three sisters." "You're going to make me cry. I have to go, girls." We all laugh out loud with very happy eyes. I grab my two guitars, and off I go.

My aunt is reading her Bible. I put my guitars in my room. I have three guitars here, and one at my mama's house. I can only play one at a time. I don't need four guitars. I think I'll give two away some day soon. I say goodnight to my aunt, and off I go to the blind man's stand. "Howdy!" I yell, as I ride and park my bike beside the newspaper stand. "I'm glad to smell you, feel you, and touch you, because you know I can't see you. How are you, kid?" "Fine, Sir." "Have you ridden any blind horses lately, John Wayne?" "No, sir. But I can say that I don't have to trespass anymore to touch, or smell, or ride a pony! I met a man who owns most of the horses I've been trespassing to ride. He has given me permission to ride any pony, anytime I wish. He is a peacemaker." "Kid, that's wonderful news! In fact, that's the best news I've heard all day long. I need you to help me Friday afternoon and the next day as well." "I can do that, sir." "Go home to your mama. You have school tomorrow." And off I go. *Thank you, Lord, for another fantastic day in the life of a baby cowboy.*

CHAPTER ELEVEN

As weeks pass by, I'm back on the racetrack on weekends. I sell newspapers for the blind man in the afternoons after school. I see the ladies all during the week. Rex and Billy Bob are picking me up sometime over the weekend. We have to work on some new songs for a party the mothers are putting together soon. We are very busy with school, music, horses, and other kid-stuff.

My mama tells me we are going to be moving tomorrow. We will be living about a dozen blocks behind my aunt's house and the circle. I've been in the neighborhood before, when I was pony scouting down the rail road tracks months ago. There are lots of kids all around. This is going to be a long walk to school. The next day in class, I find out that four of my classmates live on my new street. What a treat! We can walk to school together. Lots of kids ride the bus, but I like to walk. After school, my sisters and I walk to our new house. My mama and brother are there and everything is fine. We love our new place and we have lots of space. My bedroom is so big that I could keep a pony inside of it. One of my classmates lives right next door to me and we are walking to school together tomorrow.

While walking behind my house to school with my neighbor, it starts to rain very, very hard. We start to run, when my friend slips in the mud, and rolls down the hill into the cold creek. He's under the water and I don't see him. I slide on my butt down to the water's edge. The rain is coming down hard, and I can't see much. I certainly don't see my friend. Suddenly, I see his coat. I look across the creek. My classmate is holding on for dear life, to a giant root at the water's edge. I can't cross over because the water is too powerful. I can swim, but I'm not a fish. Oh Lord, how I wish my friend would try, because he could die and everyone is going to ask me why. I yell loudly to my friend, "Kick your boots off and drop your pants! Now you're much lighter! Pull yourself up on top of the big root to the bank!" He made it! He's out, and he's up on his feet. All he has left is one sock, his underwear, and his life. Now he is crying and he won't stop. I'm yelling to him from across the creek to keep walking. We're almost at my aunt's house by the shopping center. He's walking up the creek bed, and I'm walking alongside the railroad tracks. When we get to the main highway, I cross over to my friend. He is still crying. I take off my coat and put it around his little cold body. Now, he stops crying. I take him inside my aunt's house. I give him some of my clothes, and a pair of shoes and socks. He's happy now. I change clothes, and off to class we go. The bell is ringing as we enter the school yard. My friend thanked me. He said he was just about to give up, until he heard my loud voice. He thought he was a goner. He says he'll take the bus from now on.

After school, I go to help the blind man. We are selling all kinds of papers from everywhere. Cars are pulling up to the stand for racing forms, pink sheets and tip sheets for the racetrack. I'm selling newspapers from New York City where my baby cowboys, Rex and Billy Bob spent most of last summer.

I get back to my aunt's house and she's not home yet. I hear the phone and it's the baby cowboys calling. They are picking me up at one o'clock tomorrow. I tell them I have moved, and to pick me up at my aunt's house. Soon the ladies come back from Bible study. I speak with the girls a short time before going next door to say howdy to the race trackers, and let them know I will be going with them in the morning. "Yes, baby cowboy. We know, and we are picking you up at your new house. We know where you live. We'll see you early, kid. Be ready by three o'clock. Now get some sleep." So off I ride, like a race horse to the finish line.

I'm home and my mother is happy. She heard about what happened to my classmate and me. She's glad we boys are all right tonight. I play my guitar, take a bath, and eat before I fall asleep.

I'm on the porch cleaning my saddle when the legendary Black wild horse wranglers show up. On the backside, I only have to clean and fill water buckets in one barn. They have lots of help this year. When I finish, I have to put my pony boy horse on the walking machine so I can clean his stall. The horses are done eating. Now we get them ready for the track. I see the jockeys and pony boys out in the parking lot. There's action when they come around. All the horses are training this morning. I saddle my pony, and ride in the barn until I see horses coming back from the track. Then I stall my pony, and I start hot walking a few horses around the inside of the barn until they cool down. Then, we give them a fabulous bath and we brush down their whole bodies. Next, I put them in a fresh, clean stall. The ponies have three feet of fluffy straw with the best drinking water and hay in the world. I say goodnight to the ponies, although it's only nine o'clock in the morning. The boys will be back at three o'clock this afternoon to feed supper to the horses. Once I get to my aunt's house, I take a bath and go to sleep, until just before the baby cowboys come for me and my guitar.

I'm sitting around playing my guitar as I'm thinking of a pony, and I see my first black cowboy from my town. He's been around, but we just didn't know one another. He is a football coach. I saw him this morning while sitting on my aunt's front porch. I see this beautiful truck and trailer with two wonderful horses inside, parked across the street in the shopping center parking lot. So, I run inside of the store, hoping that maybe I can talk to him. I'm walking fast all through the store. I don't see him. Suddenly, I turn the corner and I step on the cowboy's fabulous boots. "Hey, slow down, kid!" "Sorry, Sir." "What's your hurry, son?" "I'm looking for a cowboy and you must be him." "Who are you? What's your name?" "My name is Cellulose John Wayne Jay and I stay across the street." I tell him the last time I saw a horse trailer here was when they moved big White and Big Black- before this became a store. "You live across the street?" "Yes, sir." "I know that lady. She's my aunt from Texas and she's been here a long time. Tell her I said hello. We've known each other for years. John Wayne, you must know my kids." When he told me their names, I knew who his kids were. I tell the cowboy I know his kids, but that they don't know me. I see them at the swimming pool and around town. They are very nice kids. "Thank you, son. Now come out to the trailer so I can show you my horses." In the parking lot, he takes a horse out of the trailer so I can get a better look. Then he takes the other horse out. I tell him that they are great looking ponies. "Thanks, son." Then he loads the horses back into the trailer. "Wait just a second, son. My friend, Leo, said he met a little black boy some time ago named John Wayne." "That's me. I know Mr. Leo and he knows my mama, Cleo." The cowboy says he knows my mama. He tells me to come watch football workouts after school sometimes. Then I can go and help him feed the horses. What a great day in the life of a baby cowboy! As the coach is driving away, he yells, "Say hi to your aunt and to Cleopatra!"

The baby cowboys and their parents are here for me and my guitar. When we get to the ranch, the kid with the bass guitar is waiting down by the barn. We are all happy to see one another again. We haven not played together since the big pool party at Billy Bob's house. The mothers cook for us boys while the daddies help set up. Rex has a new drum set and Billy Bob has a new and smaller key board, plus a piano. We take the horses out of the barn. We open the gate and turn them out to pasture, because we boys are going to be making a lot of noise. I'm sure we are going to hit some rough notes and the ponies may not like that so much. They are running wild and free on about three miles of great pasture land. I stand and watch them kicking and bucking out of sight, over the hill to join the rest of the herd. We boys are ready to learn the new Elvis song. We find out later in the day that we are going to play for Billy Bob's little cowgirl cousin from Kansas. She's our age and she will be here next month. Billy Bob says his cousin has a dozen horses. They are show horses and race horses, and it's going to be her birthday party. We boys sound very good. We don't know what's cooking, but it sure smells good. And just like that, the mothers are walking into the barn with some of the best tasting fried chicken I have ever had the pleasure of eating. They have also made apple pie, black eyed peas, candied yams, southern fried corn bread, and collard greens. After we thank the Lord for this fabulous meal and bless the cooks, as we are eating, I ask the ladies if they have any black people in their family. They smile and say "Yes. It's you, baby cowboy. You are part of our family and we love you." And then they say to me, "White people eat soul food, too, cowboy." "Peace."

The music must have sounded really nice because we all look up from our supper to find the entire herd of horses standing at the gate leading to the barn. They want to know what's going on in their house! We boys take a break, and cut out four ponies from the herd. We saddle up and ride for awhile. After we get back to the barn, the fathers unsaddle the horses. Rex has a surprise he would like to show me. He blind folded me, and we walk and we talk, slow and easy from the barn to the other side of the house. It is a very big house, I must say. He removes the blind fold and says to me, "Let's go for a swim, John Wayne!" I am so very happy. Both of my pals have a heated pool in their yards. The bass player and I are very, very thrilled! After a swim, we return to the barn. We've learned a total of five new songs today. We are really proud of ourselves after the fathers play back our Elvis song. Yes, we recorded it, and it sounded great. I only wish we had Elvis singing for us. Now that, would be legendary! It's getting late and we are going to stay set up because we will play two more nights this week. The horses will stay out to pasture for a few weeks. The bass player's parents are here and we all say goodnight. Billy Bob and his dad take me home.

When I arrive home, I play my guitar for awhile as my sisters do their homework. Cleopatra walks in the door from her part-time job. She is very tired and she needs us kids to rub her back and her feet as she falls slowly off to sleep. My sisters and I stay up late talking before we say goodnight. The next morning, my sisters tell me they are going to ride the school bus. I am going to walk to school with some of the kids from down the street. As we walk and talk, a new boy is coming toward us with his big sister. I know the girl. She is in my big sister's class. She tells me that her little brother goes to a special school in Little Rock for kids who cannot hear or speak. He is out of school for a two-week vacation. She's not going to school today. She's taking her brother on a tour downtown, and wants to know if I could play with him sometime. "Sure I can, young lady." The boy looks at me and smiles. His sister tells me he reads lips, and he is learning signs with his fingers.

After class, I see the black cowboy football coach down the street from my school. He sees me and says today is a great day to go out to his pasture and feed his horses. We go by my aunt's house to let her know that I'm going to go with Coach- the only black cowboy in town. She's not home, so I leave her a note. I tell the coach that I had been trespassing on other people's land, just to touch and ride their horses. He said that's a very bad thing to do. "You could get yourself in a whole lot of trouble." "Yes, I understand, Coach, but I met Mr. Leo- your friend and mine. He says I can ride any time I want. I've been on his ponies trespassing for some time now, and it feels good to know that I have permission from the owners. And Mr. Leo has informed everyone for miles around the town that a black kid will be on his land with his horses with his permission- anytime day or night." The coach is very happy for me because he has known Mr. Leo for many years and he tells me I'm a blessed baby cowboy because Mr. Leo let's no one fool around with his livestock. "Kid, you may be the first." Then, Coach pulls off the road and says, "We're here, John Wayne!" He blows the truck horn and a few seconds later, five wonderful ponies come over the hillside, down to the truck at the edge of the fence line. Two of these horses I've seen before in the shopping center parking lot. The other three horses belong to a pal of the coach. He tells me I can ride anytime I like. He asks me if I know where the Black high school is located. "No, sir." The cowboy says I can walk behind the school and find him anytime during football workouts after class. "You can watch the boys train and you can watch me train a wild horse all in the same afternoon." I thought to myself, *What a great day in the life of a baby cowboy!* As we drive home, the coach shows me his house and we drive by the high school. It's near my aunt's church. I've never been so far on this side of town. The coach is very happy that we ran into one another today. He says I'm the baby cowboy he's been looking for. He wants to teach me how to break a wild horse. I say, "Hey Coach, have you by any chance noticed that I'm just a kid?" "Hey son, I'm a coach and I've checked, and I know you've been on the racetrack for years, kid. I know the rich white people from up north who own all of the horses you and the black rooming house boys handle. They tell me they have never seen a baby cowboy such as yourself. I saw your mother last week. She told me about you jumping from the second floor window to catch a pony- that you did not catch. I know about the blind mustang you rode in Texas. I've done my homework, John Wayne. What do you say?" "Sure, Cowboy, I'd love to be coached by you!"

I'm home. My aunt and I cowboy and cowgirl update. She has been walking around the circle talking with the people. She and the three cowgirls I helped from the fire are going to take a cab downtown tomorrow, and go shopping. I think to myself that just a short time ago, these little old ladies would not even speak to my aunt- even after living across the street from one another for well over twenty-five years. Now it's like they're all in love. They are all in peace and having a swell time together.

CHAPTER TWELVE

As weeks pass by fast, it's time for the party. Rex and Billy Bob call me today to say we have two more songs to learn before the big show. The baby cowgirl cousin of Billy Bob will be here next week. We are going to play a few songs from a new, sensational, group of kids from England with very cool hair cuts. I also talked to Billy Bob's mother. She tells me that they are of Jewish faith and that we boys are going to play for a special kid's Bar Mitzvah. "This is going to be a wonderful celebration, and baby cowboy I want you to know how special you are to me, my friends and my family. Tune your guitar, baby cowboy, because I'm coming to get you tomorrow after school." "Peace. See you tomorrow." After I hang up the phone, I tune my guitars while thinking of the new kid who can't hear or speak. I'm going to give him one of my four guitars. First, I will play and sing for him. He can read lips, and I'm sure he's got feelings. I hope he can feel the music.

In school the next day, I see the baby cowboy and my classmate, Princess. I tell them about the party. They really hope their parents will let them go next week. They want to know if we have learned any songs by the new kids from England. "No, but we will know some by tonight." I rush home after school to do chores and shop for the ladies. My aunt is downtown with her newfound girlfriends from across the street. I tell the cowgirls that I'm going to learn two new songs tonight. They tell me as soon as I have time, they would like to teach me a new song. "Sounds great, cowgirls."

The baby cowboys and their mothers are here for me. We cowboy update as we drive to Billy Bob's house. His mother wants us to do the very best we can to make this a very fun night. She says we sound better each time we play together. As we set up, I recall how wonderful the pool party turned out. The kids are still talking about it. The bass guitar cowboy is here. It's been awhile, and I'm glad to see him. He's excited to show me his new bass guitar, and I'm thrilled for him. "Let's play, boys!" The parents go wild and they start to dance and sing along with us kids. Before long, some of the mothers' girlfriends stop by, and it's as if the party is tonight! Well it just may be, because in walks Billy Bob's father. And he has Billy Bob's little cowgirl cousin from Kansas with him. And what a special kid she is! She says howdy to everyone, and the mothers yell, "Happy birthday!" We know that song very well, so we play and sing, as I think to myself, *What a fabulous day in the life of a baby cowboy!* We all eat and drink as we talk with the birthday girl. All the grownups leave us kids as they go into another part of the house to plan the celebration that's just around the corner. There are only a few days left, and there is lots to do to make this a fabulous event. The baby cowgirl wants to stay and hear us play. We start with the kids from England. Billy Bob and Rex know the songs very well and the cowgirl is going to be our new lead singer. She knows the words to all the songs we play. The bass player and I just sit and watch as they sing and play the song five times. We've got it. We join in, and what a sound! The baby cowgirl from Kansas is the missing link. She is just what we needed. We already sound good, but now we really have something cooking! Rex and Billy Bob have sheet music for the other song we need to learn tonight. Time passes fast, and before I know it, we have learned five new songs tonight. We think it's great. We finish with a song the cowgirl just made up right there on the spot. We all love the song, and we love the baby cowgirl and we tell her so. She is almost in tears. She is overjoyed, and tells us that this is the best birthday she has ever had. "Thanks, cowboys. I'm going shopping tomorrow. You boys go to school and have a great day in class and I'll see you tomorrow night." On the way home, Billy Bob's mother tells us how proud we kids make her feel, and that she is thrilled that we let the cowgirl play in our group. She is certain that we will become wonderful peacemakers.

I'm in bed dreaming of a pony, when all of a sudden, I hear a big bang. It sounds like a car hitting the brakes. Maybe it's a crash. I jump up from my bed and just like I thought, it is a crash- the biggest I've ever seen. It's the old man from the White boarding house across the street. I'm afraid he's in a lot of trouble this time. As you recall, the rooming house fire of not so long ago, was because of his drinking and smoking while falling asleep. His room caught fire and the rest is history. Now the poor man has just crashed his truck into the big plate glass window of the shopping center. His truck is inside the store, and the motor is still running. I run across the street. The store has been closed for two hours. Thank God in heaven no one is inside. After all the glass stops falling, no one is there to help the poor fellow. So, I rush inside. I look in the truck, and the man looks at me with a very big smile on his face. His arms are stuck inside the steering wheel. I reach in, and turn the key off. Now I hear the police coming, so I back out of the store. My aunt is calling for me to come back across the street. I sit on the front porch and watch all the action unfold right before my eyes. My aunt and I say a prayer for the man. Now the fire trucks are here, and lots of people are coming to see what has happened. I'm thinking to myself that Rex and Billy Bob's fathers built this store. I guess they have another job now. The store is a big mess. It's going to take a lot of work to get this place back together. Meanwhile, the police are taking the man to jail. I don't think he wants to go, but the police tell the man he's in a lot of trouble. "We have to get you checked out soon before we can take you to your new home for the night." There's so much action going on this evening and I'd like to stay up, but I need some sleep. I'm back in bed and I recall just before the crash that I was dreaming of a pony. Well, I'm back to that pony and he is a wild mustang. He is big and black and very fast. I dream about this pony at least a few times a month, but I never finish the dream. I wonder what that could mean.

The next morning comes fast. When I get to school, they inform us that school lets out at noon today for a teacher's meeting. *That's great news!* I go home, and take a baby cowboy nap. When I wake up, I go to my mama's house and get one of my guitars. I walk down the street to my new friend's house. He sees me coming and has a big smile on his face. His big sister comes outside to talk to me. I tell her that I'm going to play a song for him, and she is thrilled. The kid has never seen a guitar. As I begin to play, his eyes seem to grow larger and larger. He is sucking for air. He's pulling his hair. He can't hear or talk, but he mumbles and tries to speak. He's feeling the music. He is now jumping up and down and all around. I think maybe he is dancing, but I can't be certain. I've never seen a dance like this. It's special, and so is this kid. I think I love him, and I'm going to give him my guitar and teach him how to play. First, I must flip the strings over because I'm left-handed and he is not. It's going to be fine for now. The kid can't take his eyes off the guitar. He wants it, and he's going to get it. His sister is in tears. She just can't believe that I would give her baby brother one of my guitars. I sit next to him and show him how to play one string at a time. He's so happy. He starts to cry and tears are rolling down his face. He can't speak or hear but he feels the peace and love. His sister is communicating with him. They are doing sign language. She says her brother thanks me for the wonderful music box. And I say to his face, so he can read my lips, "This is a music box called, 'your guitar.' See you, baby cowboy." "Bye-bye," the girl says to me, and the kid smiles and waves goodbye as he plays his new guitar.

I rush home to do some small chores before I go to my aunt's house. When I get in the circle, I can see the shopping center is closed and there are lots of workers inside. My aunt says the poor man was drunk. He's not hurt, but he is in a whole lot of trouble, and he may be in jail for a spell. "Baby cowboy, I'm fine, but you should go see the ladies." The old man is the brother of the three cowgirls I helped from the house fire he started a while back. And their big sister is the sweet little old lady cowgirl guitar player who gave me her only guitar. I run over to the boarding house. The ladies see me and come outside with not-so-happy eyes. We sit on the big front porch. The cowgirls are so very sad for their little drunk baby brother. "Could you get your guitar, sonny boy?" I run home and get my special guitar- the one the cowgirl gave to me on her birthday. When she sees her guitar, she is happy that I am going to play it for her and her baby sisters. Now all the girls have smiles on their faces as I begin to play and sing. After a short time of playing, the baby cowboys and their mothers are here for me and my guitar. "See you, and thanks baby cowboy!"

We are going to the ranch. We boys and the baby cowgirl are going to be doing a lot of rocking and rolling tonight. The baby cowboy bass guitar player is here. I run to help him get his gear from his mother's car. As we tune up, the Kansas cowgirl is here. And just like that, we're rocking and rolling, as she grabs the mic. It's nonstop action! She's got range. She sings sweet like a bird. She is fabulous! The sound is tight and we know it's right. The parents are standing at the barn door with dinner. They are dancing and enjoying the show. We break to eat and talk a spell before we get back into the groove. The baby cowgirl has a special treat for us. She's left-handed and she takes my guitar and begins to play. I sing and shake like Elvis, and everyone is going wild! She gives me back my guitar, then sits next to her cousin Billy Bob, as she begins to play the piano while Billy sings and dances. What a great session! On the next song, she plays the drums while Rex sings and dances. I've noticed that my friends are getting much better with their dance moves. I can really see that they have been working out. Their foot action is great! They look like little white baby blue-eyed soul brothers, and I love them.

When I get home, it's late. My mama is glad that I had a great time tonight. Cleopatra is sitting out back, drinking a beer and smoking. She wants to talk to me. My mother tells me that she is having another baby. I ask her what she needs with another baby. She tells me to get my bike. "I need you to go to your brother's daddy's job. He's waiting on you in the back of the joint." As I ride fast like a race horse, I can't stop smiling. I am going to have a new brother or sister to play with and to love. I'm at the club. The joint is jumping. I go around back, beside the corner store. I knock on the door. A big man opens up. "Howdy, cowboy. Wait here a second, please." As it starts to slowly rain, the door opens up again. This time it is my brother's daddy. He's a sax player in a jazz group. He gives me money for my mama. I thank him and off I go. It starts to rain harder. I'm almost at my aunt's house. I make a pit stop on her porch. She is asleep. God bless her. After a short spell, I hit the trail. I'm home in no time. My mama cooks for me. As we eat, Cleo tells me how much she loves me and needs me. After eating, I take a bath and pray for my mama.

I'm in bed and I'm going with those legendary Black wild horse wranglers in the morning. I'll get to see, touch, feel and ride thoroughbreds. And I'll take great care of them and show them much love. I'll help keep their house in order. It has to be spic-and-span, because I can't stand a dirty stall, and their water must be clean enough for me to drink.

I'm at my aunt's house early. The boys see me coming. They are glad to see me. I always miss these fellows and I love them all. At the track I only have one full barn this morning. That's great. Forty buckets is an easy job for me. I've been doing this since I was a kid. Most of the old boys are here this year. It's great to see them! After I finish the water chores, we clean stalls and the entire barn. The boss yells to me, "You're done, kid! Saddle up your pony. He's off today!" *Thank you, Lord, for another fabulous, blessed day in the life of a stick horse baby cowboy.* As I ride on the backside, someone yells my name. When I turn and look, it's my two big cowboy pals, Mr. Leo and the black cowboy football coach. They tell me to come see them when I get time.

Last night I had a dream about my new pal down the street. This is special, because I always dream of a pony. *The kid is sitting on his front porch playing the guitar I gave to him, one string at a time. I think it's a good time for me to flip the strings over for a right-handed person. The boy really loves his guitar. I began to teach him how to place his fingers to get a clear sound when making a chord. The kid is a quick study. Thank you, Lord.*

It's a very hot, sticky morning. I'm sitting on the front porch holding my new little baby brother when suddenly his pants are wet, then so are mine. My mama is off today and she tells us that we may move back to Texas real soon. I seem to be the only one happy about the good news. My big sister takes the kids downtown window shopping as Cleopatra tells me why we are moving. Her father has gotten out of jail after a long, long time behind bars. She tells me that when she was my age, her father somehow thought his wife was having a love affair with the man across the street. My grandmother was expecting a baby. In a mad, foolish rage, my grandfather shot his wife, the baby and the man across the street with one shot. So, my mother was raised by her daddy's sisters. I call them my aunties who are wonderful angels, and I love them dearly. Cleopatra tells me we may stay for a year or so, or maybe more. I miss Texas and I'm happy to be going back, but they don't have a racetrack in my grandfather's town. But, they do have lots of wild mustangs. I've seen a few, but I sure would love to see lots more. I want to touch and ride as many as I can.

CHAPTER THIRTEEN

As weeks and months pass, we are saying goodbye to the people near and dear to us. Sad but true, the stick horse cowboy is headed back to the Lone Star State. I will miss everyone, but I will be back. My aunt will be coming to see us when she gets a chance. My sisters are crying as we leave for the train station. Rex and Billy Bob are going back to New York this weekend for half of the summer. I'm going to miss the little baby cowboys and all of the sweet, little old white lady cowgirls. I'm sure we will meet again, somewhere down the trail. I'm asleep on the train, dreaming of a pony, when my mama wakes me up to tell me to watch the baby boy while she goes to the ladies' room. She says we are almost to my grandfather's house. I'm thrilled and wide awake.

After meeting my grandpa, I thought of the three people who are no longer here because of the very bad thing he did many years ago. I'm just a kid, and I love my granddaddy. We go over to meet my aunt and other kin folks. As days and weeks pass, my mother begins working, and seems to be happy. She knows lots of people. This is her hometown. There are lots of kids all around our house. We kids are home alone until five o'clock. That's when mama and grandpa get home from work. We boys scout out the place not far from our house. There are lots and lots of pigs around the place. When we see the old black man feeding them, we are thrilled. I've seen pigs before, but not this many in one spot, eating and hanging around in the slop and mud.

My cowboy cousin and his pals have gone to New Mexico to get some wild horses for some of the ranchers. My aunt says they should be back soon. Meanwhile, I help my grandpa wash his truck while my mama cooks supper and the kids play. He's not a man of many words, but he says I've done a great job on his tires and he gives me a dollar. My mama needs me to go up the road to the store. As I'm walking, I meet a sweet little old black lady who lives four doors down from us. Her name is Miss Walker, and she's working in her flower bed. I tell her my name, and she asks about my mama. We talk a bit before I go. She would like for me to bring her a soda pop from the store. And that's how I met my new little sweet old lady Texas cowgirl, and it was love at first sight! I go back to her house after dropping off my mama's items at home. Miss Walker and I sat on her porch and talked until almost dark. She had horses on the farm most of her life. What a cowgirl. She needs me to help her around the house sometimes. As we say goodnight, she tells me if I ever need her for anything, to please tap on her door- night or day. She also tells me that she sleeps lightly.

Cleo is happy that I met Miss Walker. My mama tells me she's a real nice and tough lady, and to help her whenever she needs me. Then she tells me to get some sleep. As I lay and pray for everyone and all the horses, I just can't fall asleep. I'm thinking about grandparents; my daddy's father is a pastor, a man of God. My mama's daddy killed three people. That makes him a killer. But I'm just a kid and I love him. It's like I'm stuck in the middle of good and evil grandpas.

The next day my brothers and I go back to the pig pen. The kids down the street tell us not to fool around with the pig man. Word on the street is that he has killed a few people. I'm wondering if he knows my grandpa. My brother, Deano, wants to ride a pig. I tell him that's not a good thing to do. He doesn't listen to me, and the next thing I know, he's in the pig pen jumping on the back of a pig. He stays on a few seconds, before falling into the slop and mud. He tries again. I tell him pigs are not for riding. We go down to the creek and get him cleaned up. It's such a hot day. We all just jump in. We are dry before we reach home. I tell the boys never to go without me to the pig pens. "You boys could get hurt. If you boys are good, I'll take you for a ride on a pony one day." We get home and my sisters want information. They want to know what's going on, and just by the looks of our shoes, they suspect we're up to no good- but we're not talking. We take a bath and a nap until Cleo gets home. My grandpa is here. He has little baby chickens for each of us. We give them all names and we learn how to take care of them. There is really not much to do except give them clean water and feed them.

The next day I go to Miss Walker's house. We work in the yard and drink soda pop. I see that she has a gun in her back pocket. We do not say a word about the gun. Miss Walker tells me she has been around this town a long time. "John Wayne, you and your brothers are going to get in a whole lot of trouble if you play around with the pig man. I don't want you boys hurt. Will you stay away?" "Yes, ma'am. We will." I'm amazed that she knew about our little adventure. We work another hour or so and she pays me five dollars. When I get home, my sisters are playing next door and my brothers are nowhere to be found. So, I go to the pig pens and to my surprise, all the pigs are gone, and the fence is broken. I see my brothers' shoe tracks in the mud. We're in a whole lot of trouble. When I reach home, my brothers are in the backyard crying. They know they did a bad thing, and the boys are sorry, but sorry won't cut it. "We've got to get all the ham and bacon back, boys." We get food, nails and a hammer. When we see a few pigs, we drop food. We have a whole pot of beans- our dinner- but now it belongs to the pigs. The baby boy opens the gate and Deano pours beans in a line headed right into the pen. The pigs are coming toward the food. We also give them a whole loaf of bread, and the pigs are having a great time. Once they are inside, I nail the boards back to the fence. We rush back before my parents get home. My sisters know what happened, but they are not talking. The boys say they will stay away, for sure, from now on. We see Mr. pig man with his horse and wagon, coming down the road. The men stop and talk. The old boys are not happy that we were fooling around with the pigs, because we could get hurt. We tell the pig man we're sorry and we won't mess around with his pigs again. I ask the man if I could go and help him feed the pigs supper. He tells me "No." Ten feet down the road he turns around and says, "Come here, kid." I look at my grandpa. He smiles and says, "Go."

The old man's name is Mr. Buck. He has known grandpa a long time- even before he went to jail. He teaches me how to handle the horse and wagon. Mr. Buck tells me he's not mad at my brothers and me. He just doesn't want us to get hurt. I know the kids up and down the street and all around our house, and they have all said to stay away from the pig man. But, Mr. Buck is now one of my new pals. I love the pig man. He tells me kids over the years have let his pigs out all over the town, and some have not been found. All of a sudden, I tell Mr. Buck that my brothers rode his pigs today and broke the fence. "But we caught all the ham and bacon and fixed the gate." When he sees that all the pigs are there, plus some, he's a happy man. Sometimes it takes a week to round up all his pigs. He is amazed that we caught every last pig and that the fence is repaired. "How did you kids round up all of my pigs?" I told him we used beans and white bread and had lots of luck. And I'm sure that God must have had a hand in the roundup. Thank you, Lord. Peace."

My new-found friend and I head back toward town and my house. He lets me drive the horse and wagon right up to my front door. All the kids up and down the road are shocked. Kids and parents are standing in their front yards watching as we drive by. I'm the only person that has ever ridden in the wagon with Mr. Buck. He's a man most people fear around the town, just as they fear my grandpa. It's becoming very clear that these two old soft spoken men have a few things in common. They are both killers. I'm just a kid, and I can't judge them. I'm sure they must be sorry for their crimes. In the meantime, I can only feel love for these old boys. The next day, I go down to Miss Walker's house. She wants an update on my pig adventure. We talk and work awhile. She tells me I'm a fabulous peacemaker, even more special than the thirty-eight special she carries in her back pocket. "Baby cowboy, I know for sure that your grandpa and Mr. Buck are bad men. I've known those crooks for years. You watch yourself, kid. I don't trust them, and I don't like them at all. You call me if need be. I'm not afraid of your grandpa or the pig man, Mr. Buck. They know me, and where I stand. I have not killed anyone, but those old boys know that I'll shoot first, and the rest will be history." As I look and listen, I think about what my mama said about Miss Walker. She is a real tough lady. She is also very courageous- and I'm in love. We work a little bit more in the yard. Before I go, she pays me five dollars and says, "Baby cowboy, I was shocked and happy at the same time to see you, of all people, driving Mr. Buck. You seem to be a better driver." "See you, bye." I look back as she smiles.

I feed chickens and do chores before my mama comes home. The kids are out playing. I don't think they miss Arkansas that much. But I sure do. Cleopatra is home and she want a cowboy update. We talk out back in the chicken coop. That's where she can have a cold beer and a smoke. Grandpa doesn't like women to drink or smoke, and he will be home real soon. My mama tells me that she loves me, and that my cowboy cousin will be back tomorrow. That's great news. My mother knows how I get when I can't have my medication. The pony-fever hits me real hard. Good thing I met Mr. Buck. His pony is wonderful, and he pulls a big wagon. Cleo tells me to stop dragging my little brothers around into every pig pen, goat pen, dog pen and horse pen. She doesn't need any more cowboys in the house. "Cellulose John Wayne Jay, you're it! There's only room in the house for one cowboy." I see grandpa coming down the road. Cleo kills the smoke and downs two beers. As she goes to start supper, I go out front to greet my grandpa. He's happy to see me and wants to know if I can help him wash his car.

We live in town, but far away from my aunt's house. I miss her and all my folks, and I'm going to see her soon. My uncle is still away, but he'll be home soon. The night is bright and I can't sleep. I get my guitar. I go sit out in the chicken coop and play the new Elvis song for the baby chicks. They are dancing around and they love it. Then I play a song by those sensational kids from England. The chicks are having a blast. As I run fast to bed, it begins to rain. *Lord, thank you for another fabulous day in the life of a baby cowboy!*

The horse and wagon are what I see as I look from my bedroom window. I jump up fast before my little brothers wake up. They try to follow me everywhere I go. I had a dream about my mama last night. She doesn't want those baby boys getting hurt trying to keep up with me. I get dressed, and out of the door I go, fast like a race horse. I catch Mr. Buck and I jump on top of the slop cans and into the front seat with the pig man.

Suddenly, he pulls out a pistol, before realizing it's me. He tells me he's an old man and he doesn't see well anymore. "Please don't ever sneak up on an old gun-packing Texas boy like myself. It's danger, kid." "Sure, Mr. Buck." "I hope you know it, kid. I've got a hairpin trigger on this gun. I could have shot you by mistake, baby cowboy. Please talk loudly around me, kid. I don't hear so well these days." "Sure thing, Mr. Buck." "Kid, I've got a pony for you and I'm going to have him here in a few days. I've got men coming today to build a nice pen for two horses- yours and mine." "Thank you, sir!" After we feed the pigs, my pal lets me drive the horse and wagon.

When I get back home, my mama and grandpa have already gone to work. I play with the kids awhile, feed chickens and then walk four doors down to Miss Walker's. I see two ladies walking across the street, and we say hello. As I sit down on the street curb, I find myself crying like a little baby, and I can't seem to stop. The ladies remind me of my aunt. One aunt is here and the other is back in my hometown. *Lord, I miss her.* I'm still crying when Miss Walker comes out of her gate and sits next to me. She hugs and kisses my face. "Have those crooks harmed you?" she asks. Suddenly, I stop crying. I smile and tell her that we don't have a phone and I miss my aunt. "Come with me, baby cowboy. You can use my phone any time you wish." I call the shop. My uncle answers and says he's happy to hear form me. He gets his wife, and we talk for a short time. She says her boy will come for me tomorrow. I'm tearing up and my voice is trembling a bit when my aunt says to me, "Get hold of yourself, John Wayne, and call my sister in Hot Springs. See you tomorrow. I love you." She knows that I've never been away from her sister for this long. Miss Walker smiles and tells me to make the call, and she'll pay the bill. I call my aunt, and she can tell that I have had a good cry. Only she and I know why. She says she misses me and loves me, and she's going to catch a train in two days to come see me. Miss Walker doesn't know much about my aunts, but she knows that there is lots of love in the air. I thank her for the use of the phone, and we pull weeds in her back yard. After awhile, we have lunch and talk on the front porch. Miss Walker tells me how happy she is that I live just four doors down. I'm the only kid she lets in her yard, and she prays for me every night. She says there are lots of bad people around this part of town. "You stay alert and pay attention, baby cowboy."

I see my mama walking down the road. *Lord, bless her.* I greet her as she comes close. She's happy to see me. Cleopatra tells me to pack my things. The cowboys are coming for me. My grandpa tells me to be careful and have a good time down on the farm. My sisters are not happy when they find out from grandpa how pet chickens turn into southern fried chicken. My baby brothers are helping their grandpa. I go out to tell my sisters goodbye. They are cleaning out the chicken coop. They tell me that they can't eat their pet chickens and they don't have a taste for chicken anymore.

The cowboys are here for me. It's been awhile and we are glad to see one another. The boys tell me of the great time they had in the legendary state next door. The wranglers broke and delivered twenty wild mustangs to a big Texas rancher. As we pull in the gate, I can see six horses in the pen. I also see the blind mustang pony standing under the big shade tree. My heart starts to beat faster and faster as I walk near. He knows I'm here. It's been awhile, and he is looking good. He smells me as I stick a carrot in his mouth and string rope his neck. I think of my friend, the blind man, as I walk back to the cowboys to saddle my pony. When I see the blind man again, I will be able to say I rode the blind pony this summer, and he still handles just fine. When saddled, the cowboys tell me to take a ride, and when I get back I can watch them break a wild mustang. The mustang is strong and he wants to go. He side passes. He knows the feeling of walking head-first into a tree. I circle him around a bit and we stay far away from the cattle. He calms down and we walk in the woods. I use my legs to make him walk a straighter line between the trees. We walk easy, and I let his body touch the tree. I feel he trusts me not to lead him head-first into danger. He is now walking a straight line. We do this for awhile. I stop, and get off of the pony so that we can walk a straight line together. He's a very smart pony. No one ever rides him. I'm the last one to have ridden him. I give him another carrot. I only wish I had more. We get back down to the cowboys, and they have saddles on two horses. The horses are jumping, kicking, and bucking as if they are happy to be new Texas ranch horses. We have lunch and the teenage cowboy is here. He has my cousin's son, the Texas baby cowboy with him. It's been awhile, and we are happy to see each other again. They bring food, soda pop and my little baby cowboy's pony. He's a fine black and gray paint named Ringo. After we eat, the three big cowboys start working the mustangs, while we baby cowboys take a long ride in the next pasture. My cousin says he has had a great year in school, and that my little girl cousin, Peach, is doing great as well. When we get back to the cowboys, they are taking a ride around the pen on two nice mustangs, that are no longer wild. The baby cowboy and I unsaddle our horses. We give them a good bath, and brush them down all over. My blind pony is gently head-butting my arm. He wants a carrot, but we give them fabulous flakes of what they say is some of the best hay a pony can eat. My big cowboy cousin, his son, and I head back home to my aunt's house. The cowboy pal and his teenage son are going to camp out all night with the horses.

When we get home, both of my aunts are sitting out front waiting for the three baby cowboys. What a blessing it is to see these two angels together again! We hug and kiss the girls. My aunt has just come from Hot Springs, and all is well. She has four letters from my sweet little old white lady cowgirls and other people. I must say that this is special. My hands are starting to shake, as I look and see the sweet name, *Mary*, on one of the letters. Mary is the sweetheart guitar playing cowgirl who gave me her only guitar, and I play it most every day. I feel a little like Elvis right about now. I'm all shook up. I'm just too excited to read at the moment. Tomorrow would be better. I want to be alone to read such a special letter.

Grandpa just dropped Cleo and the kids off. It's a party and everyone is here. We get cleaned up for supper, when suddenly someone comes in the front door. Pure pandemonium breaks out, but no one is confused- just happy. It's my two drop dead gorgeous cowgirl cousins, Gloria and Ima Jean, whom I have loved my whole life. We call Gloria, *Aunt Go-Go*. She has her kids and her man with her. Ima Jean is the mother of my little cowgirl cousin, Peach, whom I love and miss always. What a fun, fabulous and smart girl she is. And, here she comes, walking through the door! Everyone is happy to see her. My grandpa doesn't stay, but everyone else does. It's the weekend. I say goodnight to all, and fall asleep fast.

The next morning I go out on the steps, close to the street, and softly play my special guitar that the sweet lady cowgirl gave to me. I have her letter in my pocket. I will read it at daybreak. Peach is up now and she wants to talk to me. We missed each other. It's been awhile. She says our uncle wants us to eat with him. They are going to work, and I'm going to the ranch. Cleopatra comes down the stairs. She hugs and kisses me, and tells me to stay alert and pay attention. My uncle's son and grandson are here. The weekend is over, and the grownups have to go back to work. *Thank you, Lord, for another wonderful, blessed day in the life of a baby cowboy.*

CHAPTER FOURTEEN

The next morning I sleep late. I'm up at eight, and no one is home. I get something to eat, and there's a note on the table that reads, "Stay near the house today, my dear baby cowboy. Your mama." So, I go back to my room and I pray for the sweet little old cowgirls back in Hot Springs. I begin to play my guitar, and decide to read my letters from the angels. The girls are fine and they miss me something awful, and they pray for me daily. They ask God in heaven to bring me back home soon. The girls also tell me that their little drunk baby brother is still in jail. "We need you, our stick horse baby cowboy, to stay alert and pay attention." I cry for those girls, as I slowly drift off to sleep with my guitar and the letters from those angels. I'm awake in the afternoon, and as soon as my feet hit the floor, someone's at the door. It's the phone man and we are getting service today. That's why mama wanted me to stay home today. Later when the phone man leaves, I rush four doors down to Miss Walker's house. She is my sweet little old Texas, gun-packing cowgirl pal. We are in love and we missed one another. She's happy to see me. As we talk, Mr. Buck is coming down the road. I stay and have supper with her. She's a wonderful cook. Cleopatra is walking home from the bus stop. She sees me and comes over to the porch to talk to us. When we get home, my mother shows the baby boy how to use the phone. Grandpa is home, and I'm going to wash his car. I think he's been drinking. After awhile, I go to the pig pen, and my pal, Mr. Buck, is happy to see me. I love Mr. Buck even if he is a killer. I only hope his killing days are over. He tells me to go look behind the horse and wagon. Fifty feet into the woods, I see two wonderful horses, and they have a nice, new barn. It is great. Mr. Buck says the ponies are mine, anytime.

My grandpa and the kids are shopping. My mother is out back in the chicken coop drinking a beer and smoking. I feel Cleopatra is not happy, and I don't think she really wants to stay very much longer in the Lone Star State. She did not tell me this, but from my observation- she will be telling me soon. The next morning, I call my aunt uptown. She's going back home to Hot Springs in a few days, and she wants me to go with her. She tells me Cleo says that I cannot go. My aunt slowly starts to cry and only she and I really know why. We are in love, and she says maybe before school starts, I can catch the train and go to her house for one week, if Cleo will agree.

My pals, Rex and Billy Bob, have given my aunt a New York number to reach them anytime, day or night. So, I call them. Billy Bob picks up the phone, and there is baby cowboy pandemonium- singing through the wire! But, no one is confused- just overjoyed and blessed. *Thank you, Lord, for these fabulous friendships with my pals!* We are not sure when, but we are excited for the time that we will see each other again.

Today I'm going to surprise my two baby brothers with their first pony ride. I know what my mother said about dragging the baby boys around, because she doesn't want to see them hurt. Well, sometimes I don't hear so well. I feed the horses as my brothers look on, thrilled about such an adventure. I let the boys brush the ponies down and all around. They help me saddle both horses and I lead them around for the very first time ever in their young lives. I've never seen the kids so overjoyed! The boys can see and feel that ham and bacon just don't ride as smoothly as a pony. As we reach home, the sun is setting so beautifully as I look to the heavenly sky, and I know why. I thank the Lord for another blessed day and night in the life of a baby cowboy.

I'm playing my guitar as my grandpa calls for me. He's in his room drinking, and I know the Lord loves me. So, I begin to play and sing the song to my grandpa. All of a sudden he puts down the bottle. He's drunk, but he pays close attention. Tears are rolling down his face and I'm still on the case. I play another tune that the Guitar Man- my daddy, Abner Wingate Jay wrote. Cleo is calling. I've got to run to the store so she can finish supper. Grandpa tells me I'm great, and that he had no clue that his grandson is an entertainer. And, he tells me that he loves me. He thinks I can be as good as Abner.

After the kids eat and go to bed, my mother and I try to get grandpa to eat something, but all he wants to do is have more to drink. Cleopatra takes what's left of the bottle, when all of a sudden my grandpa jumps up from the bed and slaps his lovely daughter in the face, just like the dentist slapped me a few years back. I think to myself that my grandpa just made a big mistake. My mama just lost it. She went crazy on grandpa and had no understanding of what her father had just done. Cleo pushed me back to the doorway as she cracked her father over the head with the lamp beside his bed. He fell back, but not down. Cleopatra backs out slowly while trying to reason with the old man. It won't work. He stumbles out into the living room. The kids are awake now. I make them stay in their rooms. My grandpa has a blade and he's got a gun. My mother doesn't care about that. "Call the police, John Wayne!" At that moment, he and I reached for the phone at the same time, but my mother pushed her daddy down onto the floor. He could fight no more. We team roped that killer with the phone cord that my mama snatched from the wall. As he struggled to get free, I took the gun and the blade, and Cleo said to get the lamp. And we tied him down a little more. The phone is not working now, so I go next door to call the police, but the people there fear my grandpa. That's when I remembered what Miss Walker said to me many times. "Your grandpa is a killer, John Wayne. You knock on my door anytime day or night, because I sleep light. And I'm not afraid of your grandpa or any other killer." So, like a thoroughbred pony on the racetrack, I run four doors down to her house. As soon as my hands touch her gate, the porch lights flash and the door opens. The sweet little old Texas cowgirl love of mine tells me that the cops are coming. With gun in hand, she follows me four doors down. My mother is drinking a cold beer and smoking. Miss Walker steps over to my grandpa and says, "Good night, sweet prince. You can turn out your lights because your party is all over." As the two legendary Texas cowgirls update, the police arrive. My brothers and sisters are near, and they have no fear, because they know the Lord and His great and wonderful Father are fabulous Peacemakers. Cleopatra, the original cowgirl in my world, sends the kids home with Miss Walker. The police place my grandpa under arrest, and he's going back to Texas jail. He is drunk, but not so drunk that he doesn't understand me when I tell him that we love him, and the Lord loves him, too. "Peace," and they carry him away. I run to the police car and kiss my grandpa on his face. He says he's sorry and he loves me. After the cops talk to my mother, search the house and find lots of guns, they leave. My mother and I fall asleep talking on the sofa.

The next morning we went four doors down to get the kids. Miss Walker drove us all to my aunt and uncle's house. And my mother had to break the news to her father's two baby sisters. They're sad, not mad. My aunt is leaving for Hot Springs tomorrow and she wants to take the kids back home with her. They are overjoyed and jumping up and down. My baby brother is dancing, and he's got some moves! He's got great rhythm and fabulous foot work. My mama and her aunts are cowgirl updating. My sisters are like mother hens and they want information. They want to know what's going on. "Who hit who with the phone? Will we see our grandpa again?" They want a blow-by-blow update. Miss Walker says, "Hush baby girls, and please don't cry. And here's a good reason why- we are going shopping! I'm going to buy you two baby girls some new dolls!" Now my sisters come alive with very happy eyes. Miss Walker takes us downtown, for what could be our last time in the great Lone Star State. I tell my brothers to get a few toys that they like. My sisters are looking at all the dolls and Miss Walker is just standing there watching us have a free-for-all. She comes to me and says, "Baby cowboy, I want you to help the kids pick out some school outfits. I'll be right back. I'm going across the street to the bank." I tell my big sister to shop for the babies. When they find out we're not just window shopping, and that they are really going to walk out of the store with just about anything their little hearts desire, baby pandemonium breaks out in the store. However, no one is confused- just happy. My baby brother cuts a few dance moves, and man, he is smooth! The baby boy has customers throwing dollar bills at his foot action!

The sweet little old tough Texas cowgirl pal of mine is back from the bank. She asks me if I got things together for the kids. My big sister has done a fabulous job of getting things together for the kids. When she sees what all we have, she tells us it's not enough. "I want you babies to have much more. Get another basket, John Wayne. Let's fill it to the top, and take your time. I want things to fit. You kids are growing fast. Let's do this right. I want to send these things off tonight, baby cowboy. Do you know your aunt's address in Hot Springs?" "Yes, ma'am. It's 14 Jefferson Street, Miss Walker." She is having the store send everything to Hot Springs except the dolls and toys. We walk out of the store and it's like we are in a dream. Can you feel what I mean? Miss Walker takes us to lunch, and we thank her, and hug and kiss her face. She is going to cry. I think I know why- because we didn't die, and that killer has gone bye-bye.

When we finish the wonderful shopping adventure, Miss Walker drops the kids off at my aunt and uncle's house. Then, Cleo and I ride home with Miss Walker. As I'm sitting in the back seat, the two legendary, sweet and brave Texas cowgirls are updating last night's thriller with a killer. They must have forgotten about me being in the back seat, because Lord knows I can't repeat the words I heard those girls say that day. I guess that's how some sweet, tough Texas cowgirls talk sometimes. My mother and I kiss Miss Walker, and as we are walking four doors down, I turn around. She smiles and calls me back. She gives me ten one hundred dollar bills and says, "Until we meet again, baby cowboy. Peace."

The house is a mess. Cleopatra and I get the place back in order. She cooks for me, but I can't eat right now. I hear Mr. Buck coming with the horse and wagon. My mother and I look at each other and smile. "Go, baby cowboy, and remember that we are catching a train tomorrow night." Then I run fast to catch Mr. Buck. He sees me and stops for me. After we feed all the pigs and the two horses, we cowboy update and I tell him what happened to my grandpa. He is shocked and sad. He tells me that they knew one another long before he went to jail the first time. "I miss my grandpa, Mr. Buck." "I'm your new grandpa, John Wayne, and you can saddle your pony and take him home. Your chicken coop is plenty big enough for him. I'll come and get him in a few days. Follow me to your house and we'll talk to your mother, because I'm sure she's not going to want to stay here anymore." As I ride slow and easy alongside and behind Mr. Buck and his horse and wagon, atop a fabulous Texas mustang named Lucky, I'm sure my grandpa would be happy to know that his grandson will be camping out in the backyard tonight with the chickens and a pony. Cleopatra knows how far I will go to touch a pony, so she's not shocked when we ride up in the front yard. Mr. Buck goes up and talks to Cleo while I tie my pony to a tree in the yard. I give the horses water, and they are happy. As we three sit on the front porch drinking soda pop and updating, Miss Walker comes from four doors down to see if the baby cowboy is still around the town. I'm thinking to myself after she says hello to all, that this must be sweet little lady Texas cowgirl code talk for, "Come see me later, baby cowboy." Miss Walker gives my mama a letter, smiles and goes back home. I know she would like to stay, but she doesn't like Mr. Buck.

After Cleopatra and I are home alone, my mama breaks down and cries. It just hit her hard, much harder, than a slap in the face. "Baby cowboy, I've got to leave this place. I need you to go four doors down and hang around with your pal. I'll set up your camp in the backyard after I ride your pony down the road to see a friend. I'll come for you before it gets late." Miss Walker is sitting on her front porch. She has dinner cooking, and she knows the time is near, and that after tomorrow, I won't be here. She is happy that I will camp out in the chicken coop with a pony tonight. She tells me to call my aunt and talk awhile, and supper will be ready soon. I also call New York City to update with Rex and Billy Bob. The boys tell me their fathers have five new race horses, and they should be on the race track this year. Supper's ready, and Miss Walker and I thank the Lord for this wonderful meal. After we eat, my mother calls to say that she will come for me in one hour. My Texas pal and I play cards. The moon is very bright tonight, and when my mother comes walking over, I can clearly see that she is back to her old self again. I'm sure she's had a few good cries and goodbyes. She has been down the road at her classmate's house. Cleopatra and a few girls are going out to a party tonight. My mama is happy. She tells my pal and me that she talked to my aunt in Hot Springs, and all is well. "Baby cowboy, I need you to stay with Miss Walker tonight." Miss Walker says to my mama, "Cleo, I think that I am going to camp out in the chicken coop with the baby cowboy and a pony on his last night in the town. We are so thankful and blessed to still be around." *What a wonderful day in the life of a cowboy.*

We're headed four doors down to check out the camp my mother set up for me. And it is fabulous. She has a lamp light running from the house with a long cord. The pony has had a good bath from Cleo and her girlfriends, after they all took a little ride. The chicken coop is not what it was like yesterday. My mother has three feet of straw throughout the coop. The pony is in the corner, and my bed roll is against the far wall. There is plenty of room for the Texas cowgirl. She loves the set up. So, as the two Texas cowgirls go four doors down, on my last night in town, to get Miss Walker's gear, I stay and saddle the pony and ride around in the backyard, thinking of sweet little old lady cowgirls of not so long ago, who lived out their last days through the eyes of a stick horse baby cowboy. They are in cowgirl heaven and I miss them all. Soon I will be back to see more legendary cowgirls who have prayed for my return. How happy they will be when they learn that their baby cowboy is near and dear to them once again. *Thank you, Lord.*

Meanwhile, my two Texas cowgirls are back here with the gear. My mama goes inside to take a bath and get ready, as her classmates will be here soon. Miss Walker rolls out her sleeping bag, and she has a great pair of boots and a swell looking hat. I tell her how wonderful she looks. She says she is feeling fabulous and wants to play cards. I say, "Sure, but first, I'm going to let you ride the pony." She smiles and says, "Do you think that I could?" "You sure can, little lady." I help Miss Walker mount the little mustang pony named Lucky. I guide her around the big backyard, and she is thrilled and has very happy eyes. I say to my pal, "Hey, Hon, where's your gun? I sure hope it's not in your back pocket!" She tells me it's in the chicken coop under her bedroll.

My mama is here, and oh my dear, I've always known Cleopatra as a natural beauty and a very nice girl, but tonight, she's drop dead gorgeous. She looks like a real Hollywood movie star. My pal and I meet my mama's friends, and they are all a great looking group of girls. Cleo hugs and kisses me, and she tells me that by no means am I to leave the yard tonight with the pony. "Do you understand, Cellulose John Wayne Jay? I know when Miss Walker falls off to sleep, you're thinking you'll ride off into the Texas moonlight. But please, baby cowboy, do not cause this old lady to have a heart attack. She'll be scared to death if she wakes up and you're nowhere to be found." "Yes, ma'am. Have fun. Peace." As they are leaving, Miss Walker gets down from the pony all by herself, while I hold the lead rope. We unsaddle Lucky and brush him down all around his body. He's got three feet of straw, clean fresh water and lots of hay. His door is locked for the night. My Texas cowgirl pal and I are going to play cards. Later on, I'll play and sing for her. Cleo has my guitar standing in the corner next to my bed roll. I move my pal's sleeping bag next to mine as we begin a new game for me. It's called "poker," and we are having a blast. After a few hands, Miss Walker tells me that while she was so excited about the thought

133

of camping out in the chicken coop with the baby cowboy and a pony on his last night in a Texas town, that she forgot her nightly medication. So, we go four doors down in the very bright Texas moonlight, and she says that this is the best time she's had in many years. She thanks me for being her little baby cowboy friend. "Hush, Miss Walker, or you're going to make me cry." We both laugh out loud with happy eyes. She takes the medication, and we go back for another round of poker. I'm getting good at this game. At this point, the Texas cowgirl cannot buy a hand. She's lost the last five games. So, I say "It's just luck, and I wish you could like Mr. Buck. I love him, and he tells me I'm his grandson. I'm going to sing you a song called, *The Lord Loves Me.*" Her eyes are happy and bright on my last night under a wonderful Texas moon. After a few songs, I play a tune by the sensational kids from England. I'm singing and dancing with my special guitar- the one the sweet little white lady cowgirl gave me as she turned ninety-years-old. "Lord knows it's very special, and so this guitar sings for you, with brand new strings." My pal is in a baby state of shock and she is thrilled at how great I play and sing at such a young age. She tells me that she feels like she's in church, and she's gone out tonight, and that everything is all right. The chickens are really dancing and the pony sings. *Thank you, Lord, for another blessed day in the life of a baby cowboy.* "You can turn out the light, Miss Walker. Our party is over." "Goodnight, baby cowboy." "Peace." As I lay and pray, I hear my mama and her friends coming back from the party. After she's home alone, she gets her bed roll and sleeps next to me in the backyard in a legendary chicken coop, in a great little Texas town- for we will not be around here much longer.

The morning comes fast. I'm up, and working my pony in the field behind the house. The two Texas cowgirls are still asleep. The sun should be rising shortly on this very fine morning. I hear Mr. Buck and his horse and wagon. I ride around the house to meet him in the road. He's so happy to see me. He says I look really good on my new mustang pony named Lucky. He tells me he saw my mother last night, and that she is sure tonight is the night we leave for Hot Springs, Arkansas. "I'm feeding early, hoping I could run into you because I know you're up before the chickens. And here you are, like a star. The sun is coming up, John Wayne, and the moon is going down. Oh, how I wish the baby cowboy didn't have to leave town." "I love you, Mr. Buck. And I wish you luck." "See you, baby cowboy. Stay alert and pay attention in school." "Peace." As I ride easy back to the chicken coop, I find myself slowly tearing up. I just feel like I'm never ever going to see this old man again. It's sad for me. I tie my pony to a tree, and I look in on the two Texas cowgirls, as the Texas sunlight slowly shines on their gorgeous faces. Soon Cleopatra hears me talking to my pony, and she's up. Now they are both up, and give me a hug and kiss.

While my mama takes a bath, I put Miss Walker aboard Lucky and I guide her four doors down. She is going to take a bath and then cook for us. I go and unsaddle the pony, brush him down and all around his body. I feed and give him fresh clean water and pick up his stall, and that's not all. I pick his feet and comb his tail and mane, while thinking that things around here will never be the same. Grandpa is gone and won't be coming back. I get my special guitar and play my pony a song. *The Chickens are Gone, and You're All Gone.* That's a new tune I wrote just now for a special pony and he likes it. He is wagging his tail and moving his feet almost to the beat. "Oh, what a great treat you were for the sweet little old gun-packing Texas cowgirl and me." Cleo is calling for me to come take a bath. I run to open the gate, so Lucky can walk out of the legendary chicken coop into the big backyard. Cleopatra tells me that Mr. Buck will come tomorrow and get all the chickens and the pony and anything else he may want or need. As we go four doors down, Miss Walker is sitting on the front porch reading the Bible and talking with the Lord. Soon we are eating and cowboy and cowgirl updating, and slightly procrastinating about the ride downtown. Cleo calls her aunt and uncle and their son. My cowboy cousin is on his way to get us. She goes back to finish packing our stuff while my pal and I play a few hands of poker. Miss Walker says to me, "Baby cowboy, I've prayed about what you wished for concerning Mr. Buck. I don't like killers, John Wayne, and you know that. But for you, I will carry on the peace game." "You would do that for me? How wonderful!" "Don't you know that I love you, baby cowboy?" "Yes, ma'am. We're in love and the Lord is so very happy that you are going to make peace with the legendary pig man, Mr. Buck- my new Texas grandpa. Now he's a gun-packer, and so are you. I'm just a kid, but somehow, someway, I need you to say that you and he will put the guns away for peace." "Sure, baby cowboy. Mr. Buck and I can do this if it will make you happy." My mama is here, and Miss Walker walks me to the front gate. She hugs and kisses me and my mama, for what could be the last time we ever see one another. As the car slowly drives away, I look and Miss Walker cries and smiles at the same time, as she yells, "Bless you, John Wayne! Thank you for everything!"

As we ride, my cowboy cousin tells me that he is headed back to the High Plains next week to scout for wild mustang horses. And he says someday he will take me along for the ride on a legendary wild horse roundup. Cleo says to her cowboy cousin, "Are you drunk? Have you been drinking? The baby cowboy will not be going unless you, my dear cousin, stop, and I mean really stop drinking completely. Your temper is too bad and you may get out of control. Now just look at what happened to your uncle and my daddy. That old fool wanted to kill me! Thank God that John Wayne was in a team roping mood. My baby saved me from a killer. That old fool could have killed everyone in the house!" As we pull into the train station parking lot, all my Texas kin folks are here to see Cleo and me off to Hot Springs. We hug and kiss everyone, and Cleopatra says, "Peace, until we meet again." As the train rolls down the track, I look back, and I know I am going to miss this Texas town.

I fall asleep dreaming of a pony and my cowboy pals, Mr. Leo, and the black cowboy football coach. It's late when we reach our aunt's house. The next morning I sleep late. When I awake, there is a note on my bed. It reads, "Stay near the house today, baby cowboy. Your mama." After I eat and take a bath, I go across the street to see the ladies. We are overjoyed at the very sight of one another. I say to them, "Easy, cowgirls! Don't have a heart attack! The stick horse baby cowboy is back!" And we all laugh out loud with very happy eyes. The sweet little old lady cowgirl who gave me her guitar is taking a nap. Her three sisters tell me their little drunk baby brother is still in jail. Two ladies have passed, and they are in greener pastures. A few have moved with kin folks, and everyone else seems to be just fine. After cowboy and cowgirl updating awhile, I see my mama, my aunt, and the kids coming down the street. My, they look happy. They have all been downtown. Cleo tells me she's found a house for us, and tomorrow we will check it out. I call my pals, the baby cowboys, Rex and Billy Bob, in New York City. It's a legendary phone call. We are so very happy to cowboy update awhile. They will be back next month, but the boys say when they talk with their parents tomorrow, that they will ask them to come and get me. "See you. Peace." And sure enough, the next day the fathers come and get me and take me out to the ranch. It's a wonderful place to be, anytime. We cowboys run down to the barn and look at a dozen thoroughbred race horses from three states. I'm having a baby cowboy flashback, remembering the backside of the track. These ponies are ready to run this winter. They have been coming in all week long. Rex and Billy Bob are really going to be in love with these race horses. The fathers yell, "Come here, baby cowboy! Let us show you something!" As we walk out of the back door of the big barn, there is a very nice training track for the young ponies, and they also have two hot walking machines. "John Wayne, let's take a swim, get something to eat, and go for a pony ride! We've got more pastures, baby cowboy. We should ride out and check the herd before dark." I see over fifty ponies all around, as we ride through the fabulous Hot Springs valleys and rolling grass hills. I just know that my legendary sweet little old black lady cowgirls of not so long ago, and my new cowgirls, would call this *a very special slice of heavenly pie that's not in the sky*. I'm sure the girls are thrilled that the stick horse baby cowboy is smack dab in the middle of another wonderful adventure. And I no longer have to trespass. I now have permission from the owners, and the rest is history. "Let's feed, cowboys."

I go home and take a bath. My mama is cooking and she wants me to go to sleep. As I lay and pray, I think of the hay I left for the horses. Most of them are not from here. Oh, what a treat when I see them eat the best hay and drink clean, fresh Hot Springs water- the best in the world. *Oh, Lord, thank you for the pleasure and privilege that you allow me to be a fabulous little stick horse baby cowboy, and a wonderful shepherd for the Lord's flock of ponies around the nation. I must be a sensation, and one of God's favorite cowboys!* Until we meet again...Peace.

babycowboy@yahoo.com

Made in the
USA
Lexington, KY

55698032R00079